Living Faithfully

Human Sexuality and The United Methodist Church

Abingdon Press
Nashville

ISBN 978-1-5018-59779
Unless otherwise indicated, all Scriptures are taken from the Common English Bible. Copyright © 2011 by the Common English Bible. All rights reserved. Used by permission. www. CommonEnglishBible.com.

17 18 19 20 21 22 23 24 25 26 — 10 9 8 7 6 5 4 3 2 1
MANUFACTURED IN THE UNITED STATES OF AMERICA

CONTENTS

INTRODUCTION

You and your small group may have chosen this book for a number of reasons. You may simply want to know more about what The United Methodist Church teaches about homosexuality, same-gender marriage, and the ordination of LGBTQ (lesbian, gay, bisexual, transgender, and queer) persons. You may have heard about recent events in the life of The United Methodist Church concerning these teachings, and you want to know more about what they mean for the denomination and your local church. You might be angered by the church's teachings or supportive of them; you may believe them to be unjust and unloving, or you may believe they are true to the way of life Christians are called to live. Or you may be conflicted, uncertain what it means to live faithfully in these circumstances.

Wherever you find yourself, this book is meant to help you understand and grapple with what The United Methodist Church teaches about homosexuality, same-gender marriage, and ordination of LGBTQ persons. It's meant to help you have honest, well-informed, and grace-filled conversations with others about these teachings and the various calls for change within the denomination. And it's meant to help you discern, in prayer and conversation, how you can respond faithfully in love of God and love of neighbor.

This four-session study is organized around four questions designed to invite consideration and debate: 1) Is the practice of homosexuality incompatible with Christian teaching? 2) Is same-gender marriage compatible with Christian teaching? 3) Is ordaining practicing homosexuals compatible with Christian teaching? 4) Where are we now? Each of the four chapters includes background on the Bible, Christian theology, history, and United Methodist structure and practice to guide thinking and conversation on each of the central questions. A Leader Guide, beginning on page 85, is included to facilitate small-group discussion based on each of the four chapters.

The first chapter describes the official United Methodist Church teaching on homosexuality and practice, as well as current prohibitions related to same-gender marriage and the ordination of practicing homosexuals. It explores the biblical and theological reasons for this teaching, as well as biblical and theological reasons behind calls for full inclusion of LGBTQ persons in The United Methodist Church.

The second chapter discusses the nature of Christian marriage as taught in existing church law by The United Methodist Church. It explores the rationale that results in prohibiting clergy from officiating or blessing same-gender marriages, and congregations from allowing such marriages to be performed in their churches. It also describes the outlook of those who call for a change in church teaching and practice regarding same-gender marriage. And it gives an overview of why and how people are resisting church law, along with a discussion of the various results of these actions.

The third chapter explores the nature of ordination in The United Methodist Church, including the reasons for the *Book of Discipline's* language against ordaining self-avowed practicing homosexuals within that context. It provides an overview of how LGBTQ clergy members and ordination candidates are affected by this language. And it describes the calls for a change in church teaching and practice, and how and why Boards of Ordained Ministry in various annual conferences are resisting this teaching.

The fourth chapter discusses recent events in the life of The United Methodist Church related to homosexuality, same-gender marriage, and ordination of LGBTQ persons, as well as the aspects of our denominational structure and policies that set these events in perspective. It explores how these events reflect larger questions of how to live faithfully and accountably as individuals and a community in the twenty-first century, and shows how The United Methodist Church is struggling with these questions through views about homosexuality and sexual ethics.

Each chapter also includes brief reflections from individuals who represent distinct perspectives within the church's debate about homosexuality, same-gender marriage, and ordination of LGBTQ persons. Several of these are from LGBTQ persons or their loved ones, who are affected directly by The United Methodist Church's teachings and practices and long to be fully included in the church's life. Others are from those who support current church teachings. Though it's impossible to include every perspective or lived reality, every effort has been made to represent a diverse range of voices. It's important to remember that these are not merely issues or events to be discussed, but people who are earnestly striving to live faithfully as United Methodists and as disciples of Jesus Christ.

Throughout this book, you will be invited to consider the various levels of the church's debate about human sexuality, to see the ways in which many different questions and tensions come together as the denomination seeks a way forward. You will be encouraged to look beyond typical labels such as liberal and conservative or traditional and progressive, and to appreciate how different individuals and communities strive to bear a faithful witness to the love of Jesus Christ in a complex and divisive world. Most importantly, you will be called to see the real people whose relationships, livelihood, and faith are affected deeply by the church's debate about homosexuality.

This debate is as sensitive and challenging for individuals and small groups as it is throughout the whole denomination. Whatever you believe about The United Methodist Church's teaching about homosexuality, you may well find that within your small group are those who disagree with you, perhaps very strongly. You are urged to approach each session of your small group with openness, humility, a spirit of grace, and above all, love for your fellow group members. Pray for one another and for the guidance of the Holy Spirit as you read, think, and talk each time you gather. Pray for God to give each of you the mind of Christ Jesus, who put love for others before himself.

May you join this holy conversation with courage, confident that "nothing can separate us from God's love in Christ Jesus our Lord" (Romans 8:38). And may the love of God the Father, Son, and Holy Spirit be with you.

Chapter 1

IS THE PRACTICE OF HOMOSEXUALITY INCOMPATIBLE WITH CHRISTIAN TEACHING?

By Jill M. Johnson

As Christians, we are all children of God and, therefore, family to one another. And in every family there are subjects that seem to bring out the worst in us when we discuss them. For United Methodists, that topic is currently homosexuality. This may or may not be an urgent topic of concern for you right now, but it's one that is urgent for many within the denomination and has been since 1972. The United Methodist Church officially holds that the "practice of homosexuality" is "incompatible with Christian teaching" (¶161.G).[1] Many within The UMC believe this teaching is faithful to the Bible and to Christian

---

1 Unless noted, all citations denoted by paragraph (¶) number are from *The Book of Discipline of The United Methodist Church, 2016* (Nashville: The United Methodist Publishing House, 2016). The paragraph is the basic unit in the *Book of Discipline*.

tradition, while many others believe it is unjust and contrary to the love of neighbor.

A June 2017 survey by the Pew Research Center found that attitudes toward same-sex marriage continue to shift toward acceptance in the United States. A decade ago, fifty-four percent of the American public opposed same-sex marriage while thirty-seven percent approved. Now, only thirty-two percent oppose these civil marriages while sixty-two percent approve.[2] As public attitudes toward homosexuality change, the question The United Methodist Church has grappled with for more than forty years takes on a new relevance: *Is the practice of homosexuality incompatible with Christian teaching?*

Controversy as Opportunity

Debate, argument, and controversy within the church are nothing new. Early Christian congregations were actually "house churches" that met in different believers' homes, often around their dinner tables. As Christianity grew and pulled in people of differing backgrounds, arguments erupted. Some of these were critical questions of theology that had deep implications for Christians' life together. For instance: Is circumcision required of Gentiles who convert to Christianity (Galatians 5:1-6)? If not circumcision, what would be required of Gentiles who convert (Acts 15:1-21)? It could be argued that Christians today, particularly United Methodists, are facing a similar situation regarding homosexuality, in light of changing social and cultural norms.

These earlier debates can offer guidance about what our priorities should be. Although we are not of the world, we live in and minister to the world, which requires a gracious response from Christ's church on contentious issues. The Jerusalem Council decided that Gentiles wouldn't be required to be circumcised or keep the whole Jewish Law,

---

2 Sarah McCammon, "Same-Sex Marriage Support At All-Time High, Even Among Groups That Opposed It." NPR, June 26, 2017, accessed July 26, 2017, http://www.npr.org/2017/06/26/534443494/same-sex-marriage-support-at-all-time-high-even-among-groups-that-opposed-it

but they would be required to observe some "essentials" (Acts 15:28-29). Paul's conclusion in Galatians 5:6 is that circumcision doesn't matter, "...but faith working through love does matter."

In other words, we have an opportunity to bear witness to the world, and to one another—witness to the love of God in Jesus Christ. Regardless of what beliefs we bring into the dialogue about homosexuality, this debate provides the opportunities to increase our understanding of the issues surrounding human sexuality, to refine our listening skills so that we truly hear one another, and to grow in compassion toward anyone God brings into our lives.

In this chapter, we will explore The United Methodist Church's official teaching about homosexuality and calls for changing it. Along the way, we will also explore what grounds us as followers of Christ and as a denominational community while we seek to live faithfully into the kind of holiness Jesus taught and lived out.

The *Book of Discipline*

History and Purpose

The United Methodist Church's current, official expression of doctrine and covenant is *The Book of Discipline of The United Methodist Church, 2016.* This book contains the denomination's official policies regarding homosexuality, same-gender marriage, and ordination of LGBTQ persons.

In its current format, this book dates back to 1972, after The United Methodist Church was formed in 1968 following the merger of the Methodist Church and the Evangelical United Brethren Church. The General Conference—the legislative policy-making body that can speak for The United Methodist Church—convenes every four years and has the opportunity to make changes to the *Book of Discipline,* which is republished after each Conference session.

However, the first *Book of Discipline* dates back much further. Methodism was initially a spiritual movement started by John

Wesley in England in the 1720s, but it eventually became a separate denomination in America, The Methodist Episcopal Church, several decades later. After a series of separations and mergers, it became The Methodist Church in 1939. Wesley himself initiated the first annual conference in London in 1744. As Methodism grew in America, preachers felt the need to address issues unique to this young country. After the Methodist Episcopal Church was established in 1784, the *Book of Discipline* was published in 1785. It included *Articles of Religion* put forth by Wesley, which remain unchanged to this day after a "restrictive rule" was added in 1808 (¶17, 104).

The Episcopal Greetings to the 2016 *Book of Discipline*, written by the Council of Bishops, says it is "…the instrument for setting forth the laws, plan, polity, and process by which United Methodists govern themselves" (page v). It goes on to say that each General Conference can amend and add to the contents of the *Book of Discipline*, and that it is not sacrosanct or infallible. The Bishops add, "It is the most current statement of how United Methodists agree to live their lives together and 'maintain the unity of the Spirit in the bond of peace'" (page v).

Methodist clergy must vow to "support and maintain" the polity set forth in the *Book of Discipline* (¶336). However, membership vows for laity only require them to "faithfully participate in the ministries of the church" through prayers, presence, gifts, service, and witness, with no reference to the *Book of Discipline*.[3]

Statements on Human Sexuality

Those new to United Methodism or unfamiliar with its teachings often ask: What is the denomination's stance on homosexuality and other aspects of sexuality? Below is a brief summary of major references to marriage, human sexuality, and sexual orientation in *The Book of Discipline, 2016*.

---

3 Baptismal Covenant IV, in *The United Methodist Hymnal*, (Nashville: The United Methodist Publishing House, 1989), 52

- *Marriage* (¶161.C): Affirms "the sanctity of the marriage covenant that is expressed in love, mutual support, personal commitment, and shared fidelity between a man and a woman," and supports "laws in civil society that define marriage as the union of one man and one woman."

- *Divorce* (¶161.D): Declares that "God's plan is for lifelong, faithful marriage," but concedes that divorce is a "regrettable alternative in the midst of brokenness." Also states that "divorce does not preclude a new marriage."

- *Human Sexuality* (¶161.G): Affirms that "sexuality is God's good gift to all persons," and calls "everyone to responsible stewardship of this sacred gift." Declares that "sexual relations are affirmed only with the covenant of monogamous, heterosexual marriage." It also affirms "that all persons are individuals of sacred worth, created in the image of God." Then it later states, "The United Methodist Church does not condone the practice of homosexuality and considers this practice incompatible with Christian teaching. We affirm that God's grace is available to all." It also implores "families and churches not to reject or condemn lesbian and gay members and friends."

- *Equal Rights Regardless of Sexual Orientation* (¶162.J): Supports "human rights and civil liberties" for "all persons, regardless of sexual orientation." Also supports "efforts to stop violence and other forms of coercion against all persons, regardless of sexual orientation."

- *Qualifications for Ordination* (¶304.3): States that "self-avowed practicing homosexuals are not to be certified as candidates, ordained as ministers, or appointed to serve in The United Methodist Church."

- *Homosexual Unions* (¶341.6): States that "Ceremonies that celebrate homosexual unions shall not be conducted by our ministers and shall not be conducted in our churches."

- *Chargeable Offenses* (¶2702.1): Includes the following among a list of offenses for which clergy members may be charged: "not being celibate in singleness or not faithful in a heterosexual marriage"; "being a self-avowed practicing homosexual"; "conducting ceremonies which celebrate homosexual unions"; and "performing same-sex wedding ceremonies."

- *United Methodist Funds* (¶613.19 and ¶806.9): Prohibits giving "United Methodist funds to any gay caucus or group, or otherwise use such funds to promote the acceptance of homosexuality or violate the expressed commitment of The UMC 'not to reject or condemn lesbian and gay members and friends.'"

- *Church Membership* (¶4 and ¶214): Affirms of The United Methodist Church that "All people may attend its worship services, participate in its programs, receive the sacraments and become members in any local church in the connection" (¶214, similar statement in ¶4).

According to the *Book of Discipline*, The United Methodist Church considers the practice of homosexuality to be incompatible with Christian teaching. The *Book of Discipline* prohibits the celebration of same-gender marriages or unions by United Methodist clergy and in United Methodist churches. It also prohibits the ordination of practicing homosexuals, and lists being a self-avowed practicing homosexual as a chargeable offense for which a clergy member may be brought to trial. At the same time, it affirms the sacred worth of all people, supports civil and human rights regardless of sexual orientation, declares sexuality to be a good gift from God, and calls all people to be responsible stewards of this gift.

Timeline of Statements

It's important to remember that the *Book of Discipline* has changed over time. The various statements regarding human sexuality were added by the General Conference at several points over the years. The issue of homosexuality was first openly debated at the 1972 General Conference, and has been a topic of debate at every Conference since then. Language proposed in 1972 to affirm "homosexuals as persons of sacred worth" was amended to add the language regarding the practice of homosexuality being "incompatible with Christian teaching" (¶161.G). The funding restrictions (¶613.19 and ¶806.9) were added in 1976, and the prohibition on ordination of "self-avowed practicing homosexuals" (¶304.3) was added in 1984. In 1988, the incompatibility reference was softened to include the affirmation that "God's grace is available to all" (¶161.G). The prohibition against clergy performing homosexual unions (¶341.6) was first added in 1996. As the *Book of Discipline* itself says, it is not infallible (page v), and there are established mechanisms for changing it.

Since around 2008, several other protestant denominations have started opening ordinations and marriage vows to all persons regardless of sexual orientation; these include the Presbyterian Church (USA) and the Episcopal Church. At the 2012 and 2016 General Conference sessions, efforts to push for "full inclusion" in The United Methodist Church escalated. Advocates for full inclusion would like to see LGBTQ persons in all aspects of church life and worship, including clergy roles, and they would like to see same-gender marriages recognized by the Church. Others strongly oppose any changes in the *Book of Discipline* to allow same-gender marriage or ordination of "self-avowed practicing homosexuals," viewing such changes as contrary to Scripture and Christian tradition.

With emotions from all sides running high at an extremely tense 2016 General Conference, The UMC's Council of Bishops proposed to create a special commission to explore potential changes to the *Book of Discipline* that would allow the Church to move forward and avoid a denominational split over the issue of homosexuality. The General Conference voted to accept this proposal, and the thirty-two-member Commission on a Way Forward was formed later in 2016. The Council of Bishops subsequently called for a special session of the General Conference to convene in 2019, where the delegates to General Conference will review and act upon a report from the Council of Bishops based on the findings of the Commission on a Way Forward.

In beginning this study, it's important to keep in mind that The United Methodist Church is comprised of almost twelve million members in forty-five thousand churches spread across multiple continents. There are fifty-six annual conferences within the United States and a total of one hundred thirty-one around the globe. When a General Conference convenes, there are at least two delegates from every annual conference, with larger annual conferences receiving more delegates. Multiple nationalities bring diverse cultural standards into the discussion. Each lay and clergy delegate gets to vote on what goes into the *Book of Discipline*. Within the United States, there are varying views toward homosexuality, but that variation becomes more complicated when global voices are involved. For example, homosexual acts are criminalized in many countries in Africa, and thirty percent of delegates to the 2016 Conference were from that continent.

Wesleyan Theology

Grace and Holiness

As expressed in the *Book of Discipline*, the General Conference of The United Methodist Church has stated since 1972 that the practice of homosexuality is "incompatible with Christian teaching." Those who support this teaching and those who call for full inclusion of LGBTQ persons strive to be faithful to Wesleyan theology.

Wesleyan theology, including the teachings, writings, and life of John Wesley himself, provides United Methodists with a core set of beliefs which were essential for early Methodists and are still instructive for us today. Wesley lived to the age of eighty-seven and was in ministry for most of his life, so his body of work is both prolific and complex. However, his theology revolved primarily around the following themes: our need for salvation; the abundant presence of God's grace to meet that need; the importance of faith over righteous works; and the conviction that genuine faith produces inward and outward holiness. Wesley understood "holiness" as having one's heart fully fixed on God.

There are no records showing Wesley preached specifically on homosexuality. He did preach on the spreading of scriptural holiness and the practice of Christian living. In 1729, he started a "holy club" where members would examine themselves daily with 22 questions that mostly focused on habits of the heart, rather than observable behaviors. For example:

- "Am I consciously or unconsciously creating the impression that I am better than I really am? In other words, am I a hypocrite?"

- "Am I enjoying prayer?"

- "Is Christ real to me?"[4]

For Wesley, these questions provided a path toward holiness. Wesleyan theology places an emphasis on holiness of heart and life, which includes our sexual practices.

Wesleyan Quadrilateral

Another aspect of Wesley's theology emphasized by United Methodists is the way he sought theological discernment through Scripture, clarified by tradition, reason, and experience. The "Wesleyan Quadrilateral" refers to these four sources that inform theology in the Wesleyan tradition: Scripture, tradition, reason, and experience.

---

4 "Everyday Disciples: John Wesley's 22 Questions," accessed July 26, 2017, https://www.umcdiscipleship.org/resources/everyday-disciples-john-wesleys-22-questions

While Wesley himself did not formulate the concept of the quadrilateral theological method, it has become deeply embedded in United Methodist teaching and is in our *Book of Discipline*. Wesley built on the Anglican tradition of citing Scripture, tradition, and reason as tools for understanding God, and added to it experience. The term "Wesleyan quadrilateral" was actually coined in the mid-1900s by Albert C. Outler, a prominent Wesley scholar. Outler explained that, when Wesley was challenged on any issue, he first went to the Holy Bible. "Even so," Outler wrote, "he was well aware that Scripture alone had rarely settled any controverted point of doctrine."[5]

As the *Book of Discipline* puts it, "Wesley believed that the living core of the Christian faith was revealed in Scripture, illuminated by tradition, vivified in personal experience, and confirmed by reason. Scripture is primary, revealing the Word of God 'so far as it is necessary for our salvation'" (¶105). For many United Methodists, the Wesleyan quadrilateral is a means of theological reflection as we seek to understand the nature of God, as well as a means of discernment as we seek to understand God's will for our lives.

How is the Wesleyan Quadrilateral Being Used in the Debate Over Homosexuality?

Both those who advocate for full inclusion of LGBTQ persons and those who support the current teachings in the *Book of Discipline* draw upon Scripture, tradition, reason, and experience to articulate their understanding of God's will for The United Methodist Church.

What follows gives a general overview of the ways in which those who wish to maintain current United Methodist teaching and those who call for full inclusion of LGBTQ persons draw upon these four sources. Of course, there are as many interpretations of these four sources as there are individuals, and these interpretations are often detailed and nuanced. The following points, therefore, are meant to

---

5 Kevin Watson, "Experience in the so-called 'Wesleyan Quadrilateral,'" May 13, 2013, accessed July 26, 2017, https://vitalpiety.com/2013/05/13/experience-in-the-so-called-wesleyan-quadrilateral/

provide a basic sense of differing types of approaches rather than describe either position in full.

Those who feel it is time to change the polity of The United Methodist Church so that LGBTQ persons are fully included point to:

- *Scripture*: Faithful Christians can and do interpret Scripture differently. Although specific biblical passages regard homosexuality as a sin, an understanding of historical and social context is necessary. Prohibitions against homosexual practice in the Bible likely do not envision loving, committed, monogamous relationships among members of the same sex. It's important to recognize that what we mean by homosexual orientation may differ significantly from the biblical understanding of homosexual practice. The Bible has also been used to justify slavery and the subordination of women, and certain passages permit polygamy and violence. The highest themes of Scripture, such as "God was reconciling the world to himself through Christ" (2 Corinthians 5:19) and the command to love God with all your heart, being, strength, and mind, and to love your neighbor as yourself (Luke 10:27) supersede culturally bound references.

- *Tradition*: The Methodist church once supported slavery and barred women from ordination. Our tradition therefore includes making changes in order to liberate people and include them more fully within our life and leadership. Traditions should exist to serve the building up of Christ's body and the spreading of the gospel to a hurting world.

- *Reason*: Scientific studies have repeatedly suggested that sexual orientation is not a choice, but an ingrained part of one's being. If this is the case, why would a loving God create one type of person who is more inclined to sin than the rest? Moreover, there are plenty of examples of same-gender couples living in consensual, happy, and monogamous relationships. These relationships enable them to thrive, do no harm to others, and serve as an expression of love.

These observations, coupled with learnings from scientific study, should lead us to affirm monogamous homosexual relationships.

- *Experience*: Many LGBTQ persons have a loving and dedicated relationship with God and demonstrate Christ's love in their words, actions, and spirit. Their experience, and the experience of those who know them, attests that the Holy Spirit is working in their lives. They have experienced acceptance in Christ. Who are we, then, to reject those whom God has accepted?

Those who want to keep the current polity of The United Methodist Church as written point to:

- *Scripture*: From the creation of humankind, marriage has been understood in Scripture as a relationship between a man and a woman (Genesis 2:23-24) and it includes procreation. Numerous Scripture passages in both the Old and New Testaments prohibit homosexual activity. Furthermore, the scriptural understanding of what it means to love one's neighbor does not envision accepting everything they do.

- *Tradition*: Attitudes toward homosexuals should be reformed to be more loving, and hatred and harm of LGBTQ persons have no place in the Church. But centuries of Christian tradition and wisdom confirm that homosexuality is outside of God's will for human sexuality. To change the Church's teaching to adapt to surrounding culture on this matter would be to depart from orthodox Christianity.

- *Reason*: Scientific understandings about sexual orientation can help the Church understand same-gender attraction and enable the Church to minister to LGBTQ persons with greater love and awareness. At the same time, reason is more than just science; it helps guide theological reflection. Reason shows that it's possible to express God's love and acceptance of LGBTQ persons without necessarily affirming homosexual practices.

- *Experience*: John's Wesley's view of experience was much more limited than our current-day interpretation. He was not referring to any experience, but in particular Christian experience as it relates to salvation.[6] As Donald Thorsen observes, some experiences, such as the testimony of a gay or lesbian Christian, are "self-authenticating," but not authentic to Scripture. Just because a person has the experience of being gay doesn't in itself justify homosexual behavior.[7]

The Bible

Differing Interpretations

The quadrilateral is a method for theological reflection in the Wesleyan tradition, but Scripture is primary within it. For Wesley, as for the breadth of Christian tradition, the Bible has served as the foremost source of authority on Christian teaching. We know not all Christians interpret the Bible in the same way; we also do not imagine the God of the Bible in the same way, and we bring different life experiences to our understanding of Scripture.

As faithful Christians, we must be willing to examine honestly what the Bible says about human sexuality, in particular homosexuality. In this section, we will look at the most frequently referenced passages on this subject and contrast the differing interpretations. While it's impossible to study these passages in depth here, the brief summaries below provide a starting point for discussion and show what different interpreters might emphasize in these texts.

---

6 Ibid.

7 Donald A. D. Thorsen, "John Wesley, Revelation, and Homosexual Experience," *Good News*, April 28, 2016, accessed July 26, 2017, https://goodnewsmag.org/2016/04/john-wesley-revelation-and-homosexual-experience/

Leviticus 18:22 and 20:13

> *"You must not have sexual intercourse with a man as you would with a woman; it is a detestable practice."*

> *"If a man has sexual intercourse with a man as he would with a woman, the two of them have done something detestable. They must be executed; their blood is on their own heads."*

These passages are part of the Holiness Code in Leviticus, a set of rules intended to set Israel apart from other cultures. On the one hand, these verses show God's intention that sexual intimacy be between a man and a woman. A man having intercourse with another man is clearly prohibited. On the other hand, there is no specific prohibition against two females having intercourse. Furthermore, these law codes in Leviticus and other parts of the Old Testament operated within a specific worldview in a particular time and place. There are other prohibitions in Leviticus which we do not follow today, such as "do not wear clothing woven of two kinds of material"; "do not plant your field with two kinds of seed"; "do not...put tattoo marks on yourselves" (19:19, 28 NIV).

Matthew 19:4-6

> *"Haven't you read that at the beginning the creator made them male and female? And God said, 'Because of this a man should leave his father and mother and be joined together with his wife, and the two will be one flesh.' So they are no longer two but one flesh. Therefore, humans must not pull apart what God has put together."*

In this passage, Jesus is responding to a question from some Pharisees about divorce. Jesus' answer confirms God's creation of humankind as male and female, and that marriage between a man and a woman joins them as one flesh. At the same time, Jesus' response should not be separated from the question he was asked, which was about divorce between a man and his wife. One could argue that the question was posed using heterosexual terms, so Jesus answered it using heterosexual terms. Jesus himself never commented on homosexuality directly, at least as recorded in the Gospels. In the past, church tradition has used this verse to uphold the view that divorce is wrong, since Jesus affirms later in the passage that divorce is not God's desire (Matthew 19:8-9). Now The United Methodist Church makes accommodations for divorced persons, allowing them to be ordained and remarried, despite regarding divorce as a regrettable outcome.

Romans 1:26-27; 1 Corinthians 6:9-10; 1 Timothy 1:9-11

That's why God abandoned them to degrading lust. Their females traded natural sexual relations for unnatural sexual relations. Also, in the same way, the males traded natural sexual relations with females, and burned with lust for each other. Males performed shameful actions with males, and they were paid back with the penalty they deserved for their mistake in their own bodies. (Romans 1:26-27)

Don't you know that people who are unjust won't inherit God's kingdom? Don't be deceived. Those who are sexually immoral, those who worship false gods, adulterers, both participants in same-sex intercourse, thieves, the greedy, drunks, abusive people, and swindlers won't inherit God's kingdom. (1 Corinthians 6:9-10)

We understand this: the Law isn't established for a righteous person but for people who live without laws and without obeying any authority. They are the ungodly and the sinners. They are people who are not spiritual, and nothing is sacred to them. They kill their

fathers and mothers, and murder others. They are
people who are sexually unfaithful, and people who
have intercourse with the same sex. They are kidnap-
pers, liars, individuals who give false testimonies in
court, and those who do anything else that is opposed
to sound teaching. Sound teaching agrees with the
glorious gospel of the blessed God that has been trusted
to me. (1 Timothy 1:9-11)

Some read these passages from the New Testament in light of the common practices in that time of cultic prostitution and male pederasty (an adult male having sex with a younger boy). In such a reading, Paul and the author of 1 Timothy were speaking against specific behavior of the powerful abusing the weak through sex in these passages. In other words, consensual, loving, committed same-sex intercourse was not in the authors' minds in these passages.

On the other hand, it may be a forced reading of these passages to argue that Paul and the author of 1 Timothy were limiting their definitions of homosexuality to male prostitution and pederasty. They likely would have been consistent with the Jewish and early Christian worldviews of their day in regarding all same-sex intercourse as unnatural and therefore prohibited. It's important to remember, however, that these authors and their audiences probably had different conceptions of homosexual behavior than many do in our world today. We need to be aware of these differences as we read the biblical text.

The Bible consistently prohibits same-sex intercourse, and the broad witness of Scripture positively affirms only heterosexual marriage as a part of God's intention for creation. At the same time, the prohibitions in Scripture reflect the realities of the time in which they were written, which are different from our own. This is a fact we readily acknowledge, since we permit divorced persons to remarry and have no qualms about wearing clothing with more than one type of material.

All sides in The United Methodist Church's debate about homosexuality believe that the witness of Scripture reveals a God of love, compassion, and grace. The question is whether all caring, monogamous sexual relationships are a faithful response to the life this God calls us to, or if only heterosexual relationships are affirmed.

Conclusion

Neither traditionalists nor progressives want to be disparaged. Supporting the current United Methodist teaching on homosexuality does not mean that one is homophobic. And wanting to change the current United Methodist teaching does not mean that one devalues Scripture and Christian tradition. It's a highly complex and personal issue.

When you tell a fellow Christian he or she is on the wrong side of history or the wrong side of God's will, you aren't just questioning that person's belief. You are also questioning the process by which he or she came to this belief. We are all charged to engage in spiritual practices of daily prayer, reading of Scripture, regular worship, soliciting wise counsel, and acts of service as means of discernment. And yet we all don't arrive at the same conclusions. This is a mystery; it may even be a gift from Christ.

Another source of authority for United Methodists not discussed much here is the Holy Spirit. The divine Spirit is a powerful force for a way forward that we cannot yet see, and it often works through our hearts, not our heads. Let us all commit to a Christ-like humility and love as we strive to live faithfully on this matter and in every other.

Voices

Grace and Truth

I grew up in the late 1960s and early 70s. Conservative in theology, I was (and still am) liberal in heart. I learned at an early age from a fierce and enlightened mother that prejudice is wrong because everyone is made in the image of God. I attended an evangelical seminary in an idyllic New England town. I proudly wore my "Question Authority" pin on campus (which did not go over well), began a student group called Evangelicals for Social Action, and marched in Washington, DC, against US involvement in El Salvador. After being there a year, I enrolled in the school's inner-city program during a time when angry parents in parts of Boston were throwing bricks at buses carrying black children to schools in their neighborhood. My wife and I moved three blocks from where white housing met black. And the white kids in that neighborhood regularly sneered the word *liberal* at me as I walked by because I had told them that black children had a right to play in the same park where they played. Peggy and I attended a predominantly black church, and once when we had a black friend into our home, we were told that if we did that again, our house would be burned down. Instead, one afternoon Peggy came home to find that a dead cat had been smeared on our door.

I tell you this not to imply that we had it hard. We didn't. I tell you about my background because I want you to know that I don't want to be the one who fights for the rules. I want to be the one who exposes hypocrisy and makes certain that everyone is treated fairly. It's in my heart to pull for the underdog and stand up for those who are mistreated and suffer discrimination. It's in my blood to challenge those in places of authority, especially if their policies harm or demean others. And yet I find myself championing the idea that there are rights and wrongs and absolute truths ("rules" you could call them) that apply to everyone. When the church and its leaders teach that we can disregard the moral teachings of the Bible because those teachings harm people, I feel a need to say, "Wait, it's not that easy. Truth matters, and we can't dismiss what God has revealed simply because it makes us uncomfortable or may offend others who don't agree with what the Scriptures teach." I defend "the rules," but doing so is not particularly comfortable for me. It's my nature to want to be the grace guy, not the truth guy....

I know that standing for the truth in a postmodern culture will bring criticism and charges of being narrow-minded and mean-spirited. It's common now for those of us who promote an orthodox Christian faith and uphold moral and spiritual truths that Christians have held for two thousand years to be pummeled as unloving. Our words, we are told, do harm. Our views are considered exclusionary and non-Christlike. And we, as persons, are thought to be uncharitable and condemning.

My colleagues and I who work in our denomination to maintain a traditional, biblical view of sexuality and marriage are often criticized in print or in person as being cold-hearted, judgmental, self-righteous, and outright mean. It always amazes me when those who are so adamant about being nonjudgmental can condemn with the broadest of strokes those with whom they disagree and have never met. The charge beneath all that name-calling is that God is love and that our views and actions are far from loving.

Such comments make me wonder about the words we use. I'm convinced that part of the problem we have in discussing our differences could be that we have different meanings for the word love. What does it mean to love someone? How we answer that question is, to a large degree, determined by our definition of love.

—Rob Renfroe
From The Trouble with The Truth: Balancing Truth and Grace (Nashville: Abingdon, 2014), 130–132.

A Traditional United Methodist Family

Yes, generations of born-and-bred Methodists! Therefore, when our daughters were born, we had them baptized and, later, confirmed to become, as the Baptismal Covenant states, "a member of Christ's Holy church," supported by the congregation pledging "to so order our lives after the example of Christ, that surrounded by steadfast love, you may be established in the faith and confirmed and strengthened in the way that leads to eternal life."

We say yes to that covenant to recognize and accept our daughter Traci and other people like her as members of Christ's Holy Church, also stating that we will so order our lives as set forth in the example of Jesus Christ.

Jesus Christ, this very same radical Jesus who hung out with all manner of society, accepting, inviting, including *all*—not just those who had his skin color, were of his tribe, his race, his social standing, or his gender, but all those who met his expectations. He, being God, reached into the lives of all and anyone so that they could be led to Life Eternal.

Well, for years that went smoothly for Traci. All through her school years she was an outstanding leader both at school and her church. She was always the speaker for youth Sundays and participated in conference youth events. She continued her active involvement in whatever congregation we served.

In graduate school, she underwent the arduous task and self-examination of her own unique personhood and came into a complete and full understanding and acceptance of her sexual identity. It was arduous in that this is a psycho-social journey, and little did she know that she would enter into a spiritual wilderness due to the exile of non-acceptance by the church she had served, loved, and called The United Methodist Church.

This denomination no longer stood by and upheld the very words of its own Baptismal Covenant that had been so generously and lovingly applied to her when she was considered a young heterosexual. Traci was no longer welcomed into the fullness of life and community in the UMC, which uses as its motto 'Open Hearts, Open Minds, Open Doors'—but not to homosexuals like our daughter.

Being raised in the traditional church, she searched for a faith community and found acceptance and welcome in the Universalist Unitarian Church. After moving to New Mexico, she felt a strong heart desire to return to The UMC and tried to 'fit into' several congregations, to no avail.

In the process of adopting a young foster child, Traci wants very much to bring him up in a nurturing, welcoming church just as she experienced through her childhood. As New Mexico does not have any UMC Reconciling Congregations, she has had to turn to the Episcopal Church for this integration and support.

Christ's Holy Church! Please tell Traci what is 'holy' about not accepting people exactly as God created them to be and stand by her and wipe her tears when she is being judged by human standards and not God's, for God Is Love! As it says in Romans 8:37-39, "nothing will be able to separate us from the love of God in Christ Jesus our Lord." Hear these words from 'O Holy Night': *Truly he taught us to love one another, and in his name all oppression shall cease.*

So, who are we to cause this separation between ourselves and those who do not meet our preconceived standards?

These sons and daughters are watching our actions, and they are hoping to fully experience 'open hearts and open minds' that offer 'open doors' of inclusion and welcome to all of God's children, *regardless...*

And God is watching and waiting also. Watching and waiting for our daughter, Traci, a child of God, who is of sacred worth.

—Hardy and Sarah Tippett
From *Journeying Toward Reconciliation: Personal Stories of Faith, Sexuality, and the Church (Waynesville, NC: First United Methodist Church of Waynesville, 2015),* 18–19.

Chapter 2

IS SAME-GENDER MARRIAGE COMPATIBLE WITH CHRISTIAN TEACHING?

By Rebekah Jordan Gienapp

In conversations among United Methodists about human sexuality, same-gender marriage is one of the most contentious issues. Each time the policymaking body of our church, The General Conference, convenes, there are numerous petitions submitted related to same-gender marriage and other aspects of human sexuality. This chapter explores The United Methodist Church's current teaching and laws about same-gender marriage, as well as why and how people are resisting these laws and calling for change.

Current *Book of Discipline* Statements Related to Marriage

The *Book of Discipline* outlines law, doctrine, and administration for The United Methodist Church. It may only be amended by the church's

General Conference. Each annual conference elects clergy and lay delegates to represent them at General Conference, which is held every four years, most recently in 2016.

In 1972, General Conference delegates were reviewing a proposed set of Social Principles for our denomination, which included a statement that "homosexuals no less than heterosexuals are persons of sacred worth . . . .Further, we insist that all persons are entitled to have their human and civil rights ensured." Delegate Russell Kibler asked what was meant by the last sentence referring to human and civil rights. This began the first public, denomination-wide debate about homosexuality in The United Methodist Church. That debate ended with an amendment to the Social Principles that added the following: ". . . though we do not condone the practice of homosexuality and consider this practice incompatible with Christian teaching."[1] This language remains in the *Book of Discipline* (¶161.G) to this day, despite repeated attempts to remove it.

In 1980, the General Conference added language to the Social Principles that affirmed the sanctity of marriage between a man and a woman (see ¶161.C).

At the 1996 General Conference, a statement that "ceremonies that celebrate homosexual unions shall not be conducted by our ministers and shall not be conducted in our churches" was added to the Social Principles, and was subsequently moved to a section of the *Discipline* which details unauthorized conduct for pastors (¶341.6).

The 2000 General Conference voted to add the following to the *Book of Discipline's* statement on Human Sexuality (¶161.G): "We implore families and churches not to reject or condemn lesbian and gay members and friends. We commit ourselves to be in ministry for and with all persons."

---

1 Kathy L. Gilbert, "GC2016 tackling 44-year stance on homosexuality," United Methodist News Service, April 27, 2016, accessed July 26, 2017. http://www.umc.org/news-and-media/gc2016-tackling-44-year-stance-on-homosexuality

The 2004 General Conference inserted additional language into paragraph 2702 of the *Discipline* about "Chargeable Offenses," partly in response to trials that had gone before the denomination's Judicial Council, in which clergy had performed union ceremonies between couples of the same gender.

The paragraph now states that clergy and ministers may be charged for "practices declared by The United Methodist Church to be incompatible with Christian teachings, including but not limited to: being a self-avowed practicing homosexual; or conducting ceremonies which celebrate homosexual unions; or performing same-sex wedding ceremonies" (¶2702.1).

Roots of Current Teachings on Marriage

Many United Methodists who affirm our denomination's current policies on same-gender marriage ground their beliefs in Scriptures that speak against homosexual practices. For example, in 1 Corinthians 6:9-10, Paul lists unjust people who will not inherit the kingdom of God, including sexually immoral people, those who worship false gods, adulterers, and "both participants in same-sex intercourse," among others. Though the two Greek words Paul uses, which the CEB translates as "both participants in same-sex intercourse," are difficult to translate precisely, it's clear that they refer in some way to male homosexual activity. There are similarly negative mentions of homosexual practice in Romans 1:26-27 and 1 Timothy 1:10. Those who believe marriage should only be between a man and a woman also often point to Leviticus 18:22, which prohibits "sexual intercourse with a man as you would with a woman; it is a detestable practice."

The United Methodist Church's teachings on marriage also draw from the broad affirmation of marriage between a man and a woman across the whole Bible. Donald A. D. Thorsen, a supporter of the current teaching, summarizes what he sees as the broad theme about sexuality in Scripture. "What the Bible says primarily about sexual conduct is that God intends for a man and a woman to live in a monogamous, lifelong relationship with each other," he writes. "This was stated as the intention of Creation (Gen. 2:24), and it was reaffirmed by Jesus himself (Matt. 19:4-6). Departures from this biblical norm, whether homosexual or heterosexual (pre- and extra-marital sex), are sin."[2]

Those who support the denomination's current policies about marriage also point to the bulk of Christian tradition, which has supported the idea that God's intention is for human sexuality to be lived out in marriage between a man and a woman. Commenting on Christian tradition, Thorsen says that Methodists and other Protestants should recognize that tradition may at times need to be reformed. "What may need reforming is our attitude toward persons with a same-sex orientation." Though the church has too often violently condemned gay people, he says that "the New Testament is humane in what it says about those struggling with sin. Jesus and the apostles emphasized compassion and understanding, not condemnation."[3] This idea resonates with the current statement about human sexuality in the Social Principles, which declares homosexuality to be "incompatible with Christian teaching" yet also implores families and churches "not to reject or condemn lesbian and gay members and friends" and expresses a commitment "to be in ministry for and with all persons" (¶161.G).

The Foundation for a Christian Affirmation of Same-gender Marriage

Just as many of those who want to retain the church's current teaching on marriage begin with Scripture, so also do many who want to affirm same-gender marriage. Rev. Adam Hamilton recognizes the need to interpret the Scriptures and understand how they "express the heart of God for us today." We do this, he says, by considering the passages in the light of Scripture's major themes, including especially

---

2 Donald A. D. Thorsen, "John Wesley, Revelation, and Homosexual Experience," *Good News Magazine*, April 28, 2016, accessed July 26, 2017, https://goodnewsmag.org/2016/04/john-wesley-revelation-and-homosexual-experience/

3 Ibid.

Jesus' teaching about the great commandment to love God and to love our neighbor as we love ourselves. Hamilton believes that it's this type of interpretation that led the early church to forgo the clear tradition of the Old Testament that required circumcision for all males. The early church ultimately decided not to make circumcision a requirement for Gentile converts despite what the Scriptures taught.[4]

Some who want to change our denomination's teaching on same-gender marriage also point out that the Bible's view of marriage includes practices that modern Christians consider morally problematic. Polygamy was acceptable in the Old Testament (Genesis 29:21-30; Deuteronomy 21:15-17), as well as married men sleeping with concubines to produce more heirs (Genesis 16:1-16; 30:1-13). The practice of levirate marriage required a man to marry his sister-in-law if his brother died without producing any heirs, so that he could provide offspring on behalf of his deceased brother (Deuteronomy 25:5-10). These and similar passages are part of the way the Scriptures portray marriage, yet we interpret them in light of the broader biblical witness. In doing so, we conclude that monogamy, not polygamy, is the understanding of marriage that's faithful to what we find in the Bible.

Is it possible that God could be revealing to the church a different understanding of the Christian marriage covenant that could include same-gender marriage? Some United Methodists encourage us to explore this idea by pointing to the ways our understanding of divorce has evolved over time. In Matthew 19:3-9, Jesus says that men who have divorced their wives (except for cases of infidelity) should not remarry. Paul writes in 1 Corinthians 7:10-11 that husbands and wives should not divorce each other. Yet today, the United Methodist Social Principles lament the prevalence of divorce while also stating that "divorce does not preclude a new marriage. We encourage an intentional commitment of the Church and society to minister compassionately to those in the process of divorce" (¶161.D).

---

4 Adam Hamilton, "The Bible, Homosexuality, and The UMC – Part One," April 27, 2016, accessed July 26, 2017, http://www.adamhamilton.org/blog/the-bible-homosexuality-and-the-umc-part-one

Renewed Debate in the Midst of
US Supreme Court Marriage Ruling

The US Supreme Court decision in 2015 to legalize same-gender marriage added another element to United Methodist discussions of marriage within our church. At the time of the ruling, Rev. Thomas Lambrecht, of the unofficial United Methodist advocacy group Good News, downplayed its importance within the church. "Our commitment to biblical truth does not depend upon judicial affirmation by the Supreme Court of this or any other nation," he said.[5] Good News supports the denomination's current policy on same-gender marriage.

Bishop Warner H. Brown Jr., who was the bishop of the California-Nevada conference at the time, had a different perspective about the ruling. He wrote in a statement that "The law does not require anyone to violate their conscience of what God has called them to do, or their theological understanding. But, if we seek to be an inclusive church that serves all of our parishioners, and all of our neighbors, we will have to consider how we treat all people equally."[6] The ruling, he saw, highlighted the difference between the laws of the United States and the laws of The United Methodist Church.

Some US clergy have likely begun to receive more requests from same-gender couples who are their parishioners or community members to participate in their marriage ceremony since the Supreme Court ruling. In the wake of the decision, Bishop William T. McAlilly of the Nashville episcopal area wrote to clergy that, according to United Methodist policy, "pastors may not lead the declaration of intent, lead the exchange of wedding vows and ring vows, or sign marriage certificates." At the same time, he noted that "Our church law does not prohibit offering a prayer or a homily in such a ceremony."[7] His words

---

5 Heather Hahn, "Same-sex marriage ruling adds to church debate," United Methodist News Service, June 26, 2015, accessed July 26, 2017, http://www.umc.org/news-and-media/same-sex-marriage-ruling-adds-to-church-debate

6 Ibid.

7 William T. McAlilly, "Supreme Court Ruling," June 26, 2015, accessed July 26, 2017, https://bishopbillmcalilly.com/2015/06/26/supreme-court-ruing/

reminded them of what pastors could and could not do under current United Methodist policy as they sought to minister with grace and love to same-gender couples.

Marriage Discussion Impacted by the Global Membership of The United Methodist Church

For many years, United Methodism has been experiencing strong growth in the eighteen African countries where our church is present. At the same time, the number of United Methodists in the United States has been declining. This means that at recent General Conferences, a smaller percentage of delegates is from the United States each time. At the 2016 General Conference, approximately thirty percent of the delegates were from African countries.

The rights of LGBTQ (lesbian, gay, bisexual, transgender, and queer) people have been increasingly recognized by governments within the United States; the 2015 Supreme Court decision recognizing same-gender marriage is a prime example. Yet in Africa, homosexual acts are criminalized in thirty-eight out of fifty-four countries. While church law does not have to follow government law or policies, United Methodists are likely influenced by their governments' policies when considering their own views about same-gender marriage within our church.

In 2015, United Methodist Bishops in Africa released a statement that encouraged delegates to the 2016 General Conference to focus less on the debate over same-gender marriage and ordination of LGBTQ persons, and to focus more on issues of global suffering. "As a church, we are called to be in solidarity with people who suffer as a result of unjust political systems, wars, famine, poverty, natural disasters, illiteracy, etc. We believe that we can be united around these issues rather than allow ourselves to be ripped apart by issues of sexual orientation."[8]

---

8 Heather Hahn, "African bishops speak out on terrorism, sexuality." United Methodist News Service, November 4, 2015, accessed July 26, 2017, http://www.umc.org/news-and-media/african-bishops-speak-out-on-terrorism-sexuality

Retired Bishop Warner Brown Jr., who was president of the United Methodist Council of Bishops at the time of the statement, had a different perspective. "One of the unfortunate things about the debate that exists around human sexuality is that it has given the false impression that that is the only issue we want to discuss. We are actively working together, including people who may disagree on human sexuality, on issues of justice and healing."[9]

Resistance to United Methodist Teachings on Same-gender Marriage

United Methodists who want to remove prohibitions on same-gender weddings have, so far, achieved little change through General Conference over the past several decades. There have, however, been substantial efforts to resist the church's teaching and push for change outside of this avenue.

Retired Bishop Melvin G. Talbert believes clergy who want to see The United Methodist Church become more inclusive must be willing to perform same-gender marriages despite church policy, out of a call to "biblical obedience." By biblical obedience, Talbert means prioritizing a faithfulness to the Bible over faithfulness to the *Book of Discipline*. In his view, prohibitions against same-gender marriage are contrary to the overall message of Scripture, and therefore immoral. His faith and conscience compelled him to obey the Bible rather than the laws of the church.

For Talbert himself, the key moment in arriving at his decision to violate church policy by performing same-gender weddings occurred at the 2012 General Conference. A motion made by Rev. Adam Hamilton and Rev. Mike Slaughter to "agree to disagree," in Talbert's words, on homosexuality had failed.[10] Instead of acknowledging that United

---

9 Ibid.

10 Melvin G. Talbert, "Disobey," in *Finding Our Way: Love and Law in The United Methodist Church* (Nashville: Abingdon Press, 2014), 40.

Methodists are conflicted and not of one mind on the issue, the General Conference had instead voted to retain the current prohibitions in the *Discipline* against same-gender marriage ceremonies.

Talbert then issued a statement calling other United Methodists to engage in biblical obedience, adding that he was willing to perform a same-gender wedding despite prohibitions in the *Book of Discipline*. He wrote that "the derogatory language and restrictive laws in our *Book of Discipline* are immoral and unjust and no longer deserve our loyalty and obedience."[11]

In 2013, Talbert blessed the wedding of United Methodists Joe Openshaw and Bobby Prince. The couple had been legally wed in the District of Columbia. They asked Talbert to perform an additional ceremony near their home in Alabama. Before the ceremony took place, both the Executive Committee of the Council of Bishops and Birmingham Area Bishop Debra Wallace-Padgett asked Talbert not to perform the ceremony.

Talbert's violation of the *Book of Discipline* was resolved without a church trial, which could have led to the loss of his clergy credentials. Some United Methodists were pleased that the "just resolution" process was used, rather than a trial which likely would have attracted media attention. Rev. John Miles, senior pastor of First United Methodist Church in Jonesboro, Arkansas, disagreed, however. He thought that a purposeful violation of the *Book of Discipline* by a bishop should have had more serious consequences. "For the evangelical community in The United Methodist Church, it's very discouraging that something so in-your-face and obviously confrontational is treated in such, what appears to us to be, a cavalier manner."[12]

At the 2016 General Conference, the Council of Bishops proposed, and delegates approved, the formation of a Commission on a Way Forward. The Commission is working through a prayerful two-year

---

11 Ibid.

12 Heather Hahn, "Ire, joy follow resolution of bishop complaint", in United Methodist News Service, January 12, 2015, accessed July 26, 2017, http://www.umc.org/news-and-media/ire-joy-follow-resolution-of-bishop-complaint2

process to explore issues of human sexuality within the church, and possible options for our denomination's future that can accommodate or otherwise resolve the widely differing views held on issues of inclusion. Eventually the Commission will be presenting recommendations to the Council of Bishops for a specially held General Conference in 2019 that will only address these issues.

While the Commission has promised to consider the possibility of full inclusion, some annual conferences within the denomination feel an urgency to continue resisting current policies in the *Discipline* on same-gender marriage and ordination of LGBTQ persons. The New England, Desert Southwest, California-Pacific, and Pacific-Northwest Conferences all passed resolutions in 2016 saying that they would not comply with the *Discipline's* prohibitions on same-gender marriage. The California-Nevada Conference passed a resolution calling for judicial proceedings to be stopped against people who have violated the *Discipline* in matters of homosexuality.

Possible Outcomes When a Clergyperson Performs a Same-gender Marriage

No one disputes that a clergyperson performing a same-gender marriage is a violation of the *Book of Discipline* and a chargeable offense for the clergyperson. What occurs after the pastor has performed the holy union or wedding can and has varied widely.

Anyone may file a complaint with the bishop, whether or not the party filing a complaint is directly related to the case at hand.[13] There is a six-year statute of limitations on the filing of complaints, with a few exceptions (¶2702.4). The clergyperson may have to undergo a church trial, although other outcomes are possible.

The first step in the process is for the bishop receiving the complaint to try to resolve the situation through his or her pastoral role.

---

13 Marriage Equality Task Force of Metropolitan Memorial United Methodist Church, "Summary of United Methodist Judicial Process," http://www.rmnetwork.org/newrmn/wp-content/uploads/2014/10/Summary-Ouline-of-Judicial-Procedures.pdf

Paragraph 2707 of the *Discipline* advises that trials are to be seen as "an expedient of last resort" that should happen only after all reasonable efforts have been made to "correct any wrong." (¶2707). If a satisfactory resolution has not taken place within ninety days, the bishop can either dismiss the complaint if the cabinet (group of district superintendents for the annual conference) consents, or refer the complaint to the church counsel (who acts in the role similar to an attorney). The church counsel, who must be a clergyperson, is expected to represent the church and its doctrines.[14]

If the counsel decides that charges are warranted, a trial is convened. The bishop appoints another bishop to be the presiding official (similar to the role of a judge), and a thirteen-member clergy jury is selected (¶2709, 2713). For a conviction to take place, at least nine of the thirteen jurors must vote for a conviction (¶2711). Penalties after conviction can range from the clergyperson losing his or her credentials—that is, having his or her ordination revoked—to suspensions of various lengths, to receiving a letter of reprimand.[15]

At any point in the complaint process, the bishop may initiate a "just resolution" process. The goal of such a process is to develop a written agreement between the church counsel and the respondent (person who has been charged), which achieves a reconciliation between the parties. A trained, impartial mediator facilitates the process (¶362, 2701.5).[16] All the parties involved in the complaint, including the person who filed it and the respondent, must agree to enter into the just resolution process.

How Cases Where Clergy Perform Same-gender Marriages Have Been Resolved

Perhaps the most high-profile case in recent years involving a same-gender marriage, closely watched by both United Methodists and the media, was that of Rev. Frank Shaefer. Shaefer underwent

---

14 Ibid.

15 Ibid.

16 Ibid.

a church trial in November 2013 after performing a same-sex marriage ceremony for his son. The court found him guilty of violating the *Discipline* and suspended him for thirty days. He was instructed that if he could not commit to uphold the entirety of the *Discipline*, he must surrender his clergy credentials. Shaefer refused, and the Eastern Pennsylvania Board of Ordained Ministry asked him to surrender his credentials. However, an appeals panel of the Eastern Pennsylvania Conference determined that this penalty was illegal. Shaefer's clergy credentials were later reinstated.

In November 2014, the Council of Bishops issued a statement calling for prayer over differences on human sexuality within the church.[17] Since that time, many of the complaints related to clergy officiating at same-gender marriages have been handled through the just resolution process. The complaint filed against Bishop Talbert, as well as complaints filed in Iowa, Michigan, Eastern Pennsylvania, and New York, were all resolved through this process, without the clergy involved being suspended.

One recent exception occurred in 2015, when two clergy in the Virginia Conference were suspended through the just resolution process after performing same-gender weddings. Rev. Amanda Miller Garber, who served the new church start RISE in Harrisonburg, Virginia, received a one-month suspension with no pay. Rev. John D. Copenhaver, a retired religion professor, received a three-month suspension.

DeLyn Celec, whose marriage ceremony was performed by Copenhaver, said that "a more just resolution would have included some listening to LGBTQ people."[18] Her wife Sarah Celec said she wishes more United Methodists would listen to and advocate for families like hers. Sarah pointed out that if anything happened to DeLyn, Sarah could have lost custody of the children they would soon

---

17 "Bishops Call United Methodists to Prayer in Human Sexuality Statement and Ebola Crisis Letter," November 11, 2014, accessed July 26, 2017, http://www.wisconsinumc.org/connections/conference-news/latest-news/1303-council-bishops-statement

18 Heather Hahn, "2 clergy face suspensions for performing same-sex weddings," United Methodist News Service, March 6, 2015, accessed July 26, 2017, http://www.umc.org/news-and-media/2-clergy-face-suspensions-for-performing-same-sex-weddings

be raising—they had recently found out that DeLyn's sister had been murdered and that they would have custody of her three children.[19]

Copenhaver agreed that LGBTQ people feel harm because of The United Methodist Church's current position. He also pointed out that United Methodists who support the church's current policies on marriage feel harm when clergy members officiate at same-gender weddings. Clergy members enter a covenant to uphold the *Book of Discipline*, so officiating at a same-gender wedding is a breach of that covenant. "One of the things I have wanted to do on my part is to listen to those who have felt harmed by my decision to violate the *Discipline*," he said. "This is a tragic conflict in our church, and we need to acknowledge everyone's pain, but especially the pain of those suffering from our derogatory language and discriminatory policies."[20]

Some United Methodists, including Bishop Robert T. Hoshibata of the Desert Southwest Annual Conference, have called for an end to church trials related to LGBTQ issues. In 2016, Hoshibata preached that "God's love is open to all people." He urged the church to "look at our world through [a] different lens and a pastoral heart rather than a Disciplinary book." He told conference delegates that trials waste time and are "an abomination to God" that cut off the possibility for conversation.[21]

In a collection of essays by United Methodist bishops across the spectrum of beliefs about marriage, Bishop Gregory V. Palmer presented a different view about the role of the complaint process. He reminded readers that the right to a trial is important for clergy members, and it ensures that they will receive a fair hearing if a complaint is brought against them. He urged for those calling for an end to the complaint process on issues of same-gender marriage and LGBTQ ordination to consider what opportunities could be missed. "To ignore

---

19 Ibid.

20 Ibid.

21 Vicki Brown, "Two conferences vote for full inclusion of LGBTQ," United Methodist News Service, June 19, 2016, accessed July 26, 2017, http://www.umc.org/news-and-media/two-conferences-vote-for-full-inclusion-of-lgbtq

or short-circuit the complaint process that could lead to trial is to participate in shutting down a conversation that the church needs to have in a variety of venues, formal and informal. It is to assert that I am wiser than the church."[22]

How might those within our church who hold so many different viewpoints on sexuality find a way forward? Bishop Hope Morgan Ward shared how a Unity Dialogue process that the North Carolina Annual Conference has used for fifteen years has "emended" their life together. She writes that strong differences remain, but this process has created a "greater capacity to live well with differences."[23] She urges United Methodists holding various beliefs "not to be afraid of convening and conversing. Conferencing is our deeply rooted United Methodist way of moving through disagreements and disputes."[24]

In an essay encouraging opposing sides in the debate over LGBTQ issues to "disarm," Bishop Kenneth H. Carter Jr. urges United Methodists to embrace the "path to maturity and holiness," a path of interdependence, rather than independence.[25] He encourages "Christians who cannot accept gays and lesbians, in orientation or in practice, to place the judgment of them (and all of us) in God's hands." He also encourages "gays and lesbians to be patient with their brothers and sisters in the church who have not walked their journey."[26] Acknowledging that any discussion of sexuality is "mysterious, complicated, and emotionally charged," Carter believes dialogue can only take place when we follow the advice of James 1:19 to "be quick to listen, slow to speak, and slow to grow angry."[27]

22 Gregory V. Palmer, "Enforce," in *Finding Our Way: Love and Law in The United Methodist Church* (Nashville: Abingdon Press, 2014), 16.

23 Hope Morgan Ward, "Emend," in *Finding Our Way: Love and Law in The United Methodist Church* (Nashville: Abingdon Press, 2014), 20.

24 Ibid., 29.

25 Kenneth H. Carter, "Disarm," in *Finding Our Way: Love and Law in The United Methodist Church* (Nashville: Abingdon Press, 2014), 59.

26 Ibid., 62.

27 Ibid.

Voices

Biblical Obedience

Across the connection, many leaders insist that church laws must be upheld, especially by bishops. I agree with this claim as a general principle. I spent all my life supporting and defending the actions and decisions of our General Conference. I love my church. I will always be grateful for the many opportunities and privileges my church granted me to witness and serve in places throughout the connection and around the world. Through National and World Councils of Churches, I have represented my church in ecumenical delegations to heads of state and churches in more than twenty countries, including places such as Cuba, South Africa, North Korea, and Iraq. I have led and been involved in religious pilgrimages to visit the Pope, the Russian Orthodox Church in Moscow, and churches in other places. In all these situations and occasions, I was proud to represent and defend my church and to proclaim the stand and position of our church regarding democracy, freedom, and justice. The United Methodist Church has done and continues to do great things around the world.

Yet there comes a time when the justice we proclaim beyond our church to the world must be made manifest in our relationships with each other. While I believe in the democratic principle of majority rule, the Bible also says "Don't take sides with important people to do wrong" (Exod 23:2) or to put it another way, "You shall not follow a majority in wrongdoing" (NRSV).

It is time for people of faith in our church to remember their baptismal vows. One of the baptismal vows reads as follows: "Do you accept the freedom and power God gives you to resist evil, injustice, and oppression in whatever forms they present themselves?" You or someone on your behalf answered, "I do" (The United Methodist Hymnal, p. 34). Even as an infant, when our parents or sponsors responded for us, that does not let us out of this solemn promise. Each time the "Reaffirmation of the Baptismal Covenant" is celebrated in our congregation, the elder at the appropriate point calls on the congregation to "remember your baptism and be thankful" (The United Methodist Hymnal, p. 52). It is time for members of the faithful in our church to remember their baptism and do what is right, even if that means rejecting and defying the unjust laws of our church.

The derogatory language and the discriminatory laws against LGBT sisters and brothers in our church are wrong and should no longer deserve our loyalty and support. We are called to act and live as though they do not exist.

—Melvin G. Talbert, Retired Bishop, The United Methodist Church
From "Disobey (Biblical Obedience)," in *Finding Our Way: Love and Law in The United Methodist Church* (Nashville: Abingdon, 2014), 43–44.

The Cost of Dis-order

Passionate advocates for change to the United Methodist prohibition against same-gender marriages (*Book of Discipline*, ¶2702.1.b), who act out a conviction of biblical obedience, have chosen to stand trial and risk losing their status as an ordained clergyperson in The United Methodist Church.

Actions of courageous and prophetic civil disobedience are a part of our deepest faith convictions. We affirm that biblical obedience is a calling over and above civil and church laws. Yet standing courageously on the ground of biblical obedience does not settle the issue. First of all, there is sharp and deep disagreement in the life of the church as to whether or not violation of the church's prohibition on same-gender marriages is actually based on a biblical faith. In facing the issue of same-gender marriage, we experience deep division over what it means to be biblically obedient. It is not obvious to a simple majority of the church (as demonstrated in repeated General Conference votes) that refusing to obey church law is being biblically obedient.

Secondly, it should be carefully noted that when civil disobedience is invoked, Christians have been willing to bear the penalty for such disobedience. This has long been a principle of civil disobedience. The need for order is not ignored but rather embraced on a higher level through the witness of being willing to face the penalty incurred. Presently, the position of biblical obedience, which evokes actions by some of civil disobedience against church law, is corrupted by the lack of meaningful penalties applied to those engaging in disobeying church law. It is now acceptable for some advocates, some church juries, and some bishops to settle for a twenty-four-hour suspension of the guilty clergyperson. Such a meaningless level of accountability has the effect of giving a person an extra day off for violating church law established by General Conference. Such actions offend the very integrity of the advocated biblical obedience.

Thirdly, the cost of dis-order in the life of the church is heightened in multiple ways. As indicated in the prior paragraph, the integrity of the witness against what is perceived to be biblically unfaithful is itself cheapened. More significantly, the church's discipline is itself under attack. The concept of covenant is degraded. Put bluntly, people (clergy, laity, and churches) that refuse to pay sections of their apportionment are often directly challenged for a failure to abide by our disciplinary covenant (church law), while many who break covenant and discipline in defense of their position (a minority position in the life of the church) on same-gender marriage are given what amounts to a free pass. It appears that our disciplinary covenant is applied to some but not others. Some people make statements such as, "if the *Discipline* doesn't apply to them, why should I have to follow it?"

Apportionments should not become a weapon, because it is wrong to use this issue to harm ministry to persons in need. Failure to realize the connection is naive at best and casually reckless at worst.

There is a high price tag to dis-order in the church. Covenant promises are compromised. Injustice becomes the charge by multiple parties, which leads to a culture of victimization. Missional resources are diverted or depleted. The ultimate cost of dis-order may be The United Methodist Church itself. The high cost of dis-order challenges us to find a different way.

—J. Michael Lowry, Bishop of the Fort Worth Episcopal Area of The United Methodist Church

From "Order," in *Finding Our Way: Love and Law in The United Methodist Church* (Nashville: Abingdon, 2014), 75–76.

Chapter 3

IS ORDAINING PRACTICING HOMOSEXUALS COMPATIBLE WITH CHRISTIAN TEACHING?

By Dave Barnhart

When I felt God's call to ministry more than twenty-five years ago, I was resistant to the notion for several reasons. I wanted to travel and be wealthy. I was afraid I wouldn't get dates when women found out that I wanted to be a pastor. I was afraid of having a bishop tell me where to go—what we United Methodists call itinerant ministry. And I did not relish the idea of living in a "fishbowl," with all my activities publicly scrutinized.

Now, I look back on those reservations with amusement. I have traveled all over to study and do mission work. I've been married for twenty-three of those twenty-five years to a woman I love deeply. As for itinerant ministry, I've voluntarily chosen to be a modern-day circuit rider and serve wherever the bishop appoints me. And the fishbowl? Well, everyone's on social media these days.

And in the ways that matter—friendship and grace—I feel ridiculously wealthy.

Many pastors feel they have to put on a mask in front of their congregation: they have to act like they don't lose their temper or cuss in traffic, they have to dress in appropriately dull clothing, and they have to say diplomatic things to difficult people. But for me, being a pastor has been one of the greatest blessings of my life. It has changed me, I hope, into a more authentic and Christ-like version of myself. It is (usually) more of a joy than a burden. I have found that we all have a call to live a Christian life and serve in the world, and becoming a pastor has led me to a richer fulfillment of that call than I would have experienced otherwise.

This is, in fact, how the *Book of Discipline* approaches ordained ministry, which is in paragraph 301:

> Ministry in the Christian church is derived from the ministry of Christ, who calls all persons to receive God's gift of salvation and follow in the way of love and service…. The whole church [including laypersons, or non-clergy] receives and accepts this call, and all Christians participate in this continuing ministry (¶301.1).

Although all baptized Christians are "ministers," some of us are set apart for *ordained* ministry:

> Within the church community, there are persons whose gifts, evidence of God's grace, and promise of future usefulness are affirmed by the community, and who respond to God's call by offering themselves in leadership as set-apart ministers, ordained and licensed (¶301.2).

These Christian leaders must go through a long process of discernment, vetting, interviewing, and voting (by district committees and Boards of Ordained Ministry), which culminates in them being licensed or ordained by the bishop at their annual conference. The road to ordination takes several years, and licensing takes serious commitment as well.

In personal conduct, ordained clergy are supposed to dedicate themselves to "the highest ideals of the Christian life" (¶304.2). The *Discipline* says they should therefore

> ...agree to exercise responsible self-control by personal habits conducive to bodily health, mental and emotional maturity, integrity in all personal relationships, fidelity in marriage and celibacy in singleness, social responsibility, and growth in grace and in the knowledge and love of God (¶304.2).

Self-Avowed and Practicing

Since 1984, this emphasis on personal conduct among clergy members has included a prohibition against homosexual practice. Paragraph 304.3 of the *Book of Discipline* currently reads as follows:

> While persons set apart by the Church for ordained ministry are subject to all the frailties of the human condition and the pressures of society, they are required to maintain the highest standards of holy living in the world. **The practice of homosexuality is incompatible with Christian teaching. Therefore self-avowed practicing homosexuals are not to be certified as candidates, ordained as ministers, or appointed to serve in The United Methodist Church (¶304.3).**[1]

A footnote at this point in the *Discipline* clarifies that "self-avowed practicing homosexual" means that one "openly acknowledges to a bishop, district superintendent, district committee of ordained ministry, Board of Ordained Ministry, or clergy session that the person is a practicing homosexual." In other words, homosexuality may not be insinuated or conjectured by others, but must be admitted and professed by the individual. Likewise someone must be "practicing" because it's about behavior and not just desire. It's worth noting that the language against ordaining or appointing

---

1 The actual wording added in 1984 is slightly different from what appears in the current *Book of Discipline*: "Since the practice of homosexuality is incompatible with Christian teaching, self-avowed practicing homosexuals are not to be accepted as candidates, ordained as ministers, or appointed to serve in The United Methodist Church" (*The Book of Discipline of The United Methodist Church*, 1984 [Nashville: The United Methodist Publishing House, 1984], ¶402.2).

"self-avowed practicing homosexuals" was passed by a relatively narrow margin, 525-442, and that a similar change had been proposed at the 1980 General Conference and failed to pass at that time. These facts underscore how divided the United Methodist Church has been on matters of ordaining gay and lesbian persons.

Some who support the church's current policies regarding ordination do not see a problem with this language. If the practice of homosexuality is indeed incompatible with Christian teaching, as the church officially holds, then it's a practice that ordained ministers in the Church should be expected to avoid. Those who support the current policies regard homosexual practice as an instance of sexual immorality, like any other sexual practice outside of monogamous, heterosexual marriage. In this view, ordaining someone who is a "practicing homosexual" would be like ordaining someone practicing adultery. The *Book of Discipline* doesn't specifically name every practice that might be contrary to the standards of holy living expected of our ministers. But many feel it is necessary to identify the practice of homosexuality as it does in paragraph 304, since it has been such a controversial matter within the denomination.

For many who favor full inclusion of LGBTQ persons and want to see the *Discipline* changed, this language in paragraph 304 is a deal-breaker that reveals an unwillingness to dialogue about human sexuality. Many who favor inclusion compare this situation to the "Don't Ask, Don't Tell" policy in the United States military, which was repealed in 2010. They point out that we do, in fact, ordain gay and lesbian persons as long as they remain quiet. The fact that these clergy cannot speak out about their own lives or advocate for inclusion without fear of punishment is, to those who favor ordination of LGBTQ persons, a form of oppression. They might also note that now that same-gender marriage is legal in the United States, being married to another person of the same gender is evidence of "practicing," but cohabiting (living together) is not—effectively punishing those who choose to solemnize their relationship with a legal marriage.

The use of the word "homosexual" is also contested. Most lesbian and gay persons prefer to be referred to as lesbian or gay. They point out that the word "homosexual" implies it's all about sex—not intimacy, commitment, or building a life and family. Many say that they knew they were different well before adolescence, before there was anything "sexual" about their attraction. We do not likewise refer to straight people as "self-avowed practicing heterosexuals."

It's worth noting that the *Discipline's* language does not address people who are transgender, intersex, or nonbinary.[2] While the debate about human sexuality in The United Methodist Church has largely centered on same-sex relations, this leads to uncertainty about how to approach the ordination of a transgender candidate.

Ordained and Licensed Ministry in The United Methodist Church

In The United Methodist Church, there are two "orders" of ordained clergy: deacons and elders. Deacons are ordained to Word, Service, Compassion, and Justice. They are not part of the itinerant system, but find their own place of ministry to which they are appointed by a bishop. Some serve on church staff, while others serve in nonprofit organizations or other ministry contexts. Elders are ordained to Word, Sacrament, Order, and Service. They are appointed by a bishop and are in charge of leading the spiritual and temporal affairs of the church. They serve in itinerant ministry, meaning that they commit to serving wherever the bishop appoints them. The United Methodist Church also has *licensed local pastors*, who are not ordained but are appointed to preach, conduct worship, and perform pastoral duties at a particular church or group of churches.

---

2 "Intersex" refers to individuals whose physical anatomy doesn't correspond to the typical definitions of male and female bodies. "Nonbinary" refers to gender identities that do not correspond with the typical definitions of masculine and feminine.

These groups of clergy are likewise bound "in covenant of mutual care and accountability with all those who share their ordination." The *Discipline* goes on to say, "The covenant of ordained ministry is a lifetime commitment, and those who enter into it dedicate their whole lives to the personal and spiritual disciplines it requires" (¶303.3). This covenant and its interpretation are also points of contention in the debate over ordination of LGBTQ persons.

A Shared Covenant

The Board of Ordained Ministry

In The United Methodist Church, after graduate-level education and some years of field experience, pastors-to-be must be interviewed and voted on by the Board of Ordained Ministry in their annual conference. This board is made up of some of their clergy peers as well as some laypersons, and they are to "vote prayerfully based on personal judgment of the applicant's gifts, evidence of God's grace, and promise of future usefulness for the mission of the Church." At the same time, they are to bear in mind the "minimum requirements" that the General Conference has established for ordination, which include the prohibition against ordaining self-avowed practicing homosexuals (¶304.5).

I've had the pleasure of serving on my annual conference's Board of Ordained Ministry. My fellow members and I talk candidly and thoughtfully about each candidate's strengths for ministry and what leadership in the church looks like. What consumes most of our discussion is not the ideological bent of candidates, or whether they are conservative or liberal, but whether or not they can garner trust, interpret Scripture deftly, or theologize as easily under pressure in an Administrative Board meeting as they can from the pulpit.

When it comes to the ordination of gay, lesbian, or transgender persons, some Boards of Ordained Ministry have experienced tension between the *Book of Discipline*'s "minimum requirements" and their own prayerful "personal judgment of the applicant's gifts, evidence of God's grace, and promise of future usefulness for the mission of the Church." Their personal judgments, in other words, lead them to determine that certain gay, lesbian, or transgender individuals exhibit gifts, grace, and promise, and should therefore be certified, ordained, and appointed. There have been several cases through the years of openly gay or lesbian candidates seeking ordination. In many instances, rather than denying ordination, Boards of Ordained Ministry have voted to ordain these candidates despite the *Book of Discipline's* requirements. Some have even openly stated their intention to disregard these requirements in making recommendations about ordination.

In May of 2016, fifteen New York clergy and clergy candidates came out as gay on the same day. A few days later, the Pacific-Northwest Board of Ordained Ministry publicly stated their affirmation that "people of all sexual orientations and gender identities" could meet the qualifications for ordination. They joined the Baltimore-Washington and New York Boards of Ordained Ministry in saying they would no longer make sexual orientation or gender identity an issue for candidates. In 2016, at least eight annual conferences took some action toward ordination, commissioning, or election of LGBTQ clergy.

In response, the South Georgia Annual Conference passed a motion to ask their bishop not to receive any clergy from another conference who publicly expressed an intention not to uphold the language in the *Book of Discipline* regarding human sexuality. Although resolutions are not binding, this action expressed the South Georgia Annual Conference's desire to maintain the standards for ministry in the *Discipline* regarding human sexuality.

In April of 2017, the Judicial Council ruled that in spite of the statements from the Boards of Ordained Ministry, these boards must "make a full inquiry as to the fitness of the candidate" as stated in the *Book of Discipline* (¶635.2h). In other words, the Boards of Ordained Ministry must examine the candidates in light of all relevant paragraphs of the *Book of Discipline*, including those related to human sexuality. The council went on to say that "There are a variety of methods to accomplish this investigative responsibility, ranging from evaluating written exams, conducting personal interviews, to reading social media postings of candidates."[3] In another ruling, the Judicial Council said that boards cannot choose to ignore candidates' own statements about their sexual orientation and practice, or about their celibacy in singleness and fidelity in marriage.[4] They cannot legally recommend any candidate whom they know to be in violation of the requirements of the *Discipline*. In spite of these decisions, several boards reaffirmed their original statements, so at least for now the decisions have not resolved the tension within the denomination.

Historic Challenges

In July of 2016, Karen Oliveto became the first openly gay bishop to be elected in The United Methodist Church. United Methodist bishops are elected and consecrated by jurisdictional conferences in the United States and central conferences in other parts of the world. These jurisdictional and central conferences are regional groupings of annual conferences, and they meet once every four years. Part of their business at these meetings is to elect new bishops.

In their 2016 meeting, delegates from the Western Jurisdiction (made up of several annual conferences in the western United States) elected and consecrated Karen Oliveto as a bishop. Oliveto has been married to her wife since 2014 and has been a longtime advocate of gay rights. At the time of her election, she served Glide Memorial Church in San Francisco (one of the largest United Methodist congregations), and had also served as an associate dean at the Pacific School of Religion. She was the first openly gay person to be elected as a bishop in The United Methodist Church.

Another jurisdiction, the South Central Jurisdiction in the southern United States, quickly contested Oliveto's election and consecration. Rev. Keith Boyette, who represented the South Central Jurisdiction, claimed

---

3 Judicial Council Decision No. 1344, http://www.umc.org/decisions/71963

4 Judicial Council Decision No. 1343, http://www.umc.org/decisions/71962

that "their act in electing that person was null, void, and of no effect."[5] Boyette is the president of the Wesleyan Covenant Association, an organization of more traditional evangelical individuals and congregations in The United Methodist Church. The Wesleyan Covenant Association also issued a statement regarding Oliveto's election and consecration as bishop, saying, "There can be no sustainable future for The United Methodist Church, as currently structured, without accountability for all our clergy, including our episcopal leaders."[6]

In a 6–3 decision, the Judicial Council ruled in April 2017 that the consecration of Bishop Oliveto was in violation of church law. Her marriage to her spouse, they said, was evidence of being a "self-avowed practicing homosexual," and they ruled that both she and those who consecrated her had violated their "commitment to abide by and uphold the church's definition of marriage and stance on homosexuality." But they also ruled that she "remains in good standing," pending any complaints against her or those who consecrated her—which would be resolved in the Western Jurisdiction. She remains bishop for the time being.[7]

Oliveto's election and consecration as bishop and the related Judicial Council ruling have heightened the tension in the debate about ordaining "self-avowed practicing homosexuals" in The United Methodist Church.

Using the Quadrilateral to Address the Ordination Question

In the first chapter of this book, Jill M. Johnson discussed the idea of the Wesleyan Quadrilateral as a means of engaging in theological

---

5 Laurie Goodstein, "Methodist High Court Rejects First Openly Gay Bishop's Consecration," *The New York Times*, April 28, 2017, accessed July 26, 2017, https://www.nytimes.com/2017/04/28/us/methodist-high-court-rejects-first-gay-bishops-consecration.html?_r=1

6 "Wesleyan Covenant Association Statement on Judicial Council Decision Involving Bishop Karen Oliveto," accessed July 27, 2017, Wesleyancovenant.org/wca-statements-and-beliefs,/#-diveto

7 Judicial Council Decision # 1341, http://www.umc.org/decisions/71953.

reflection. These four theological sources of Scripture, Tradition, Reason, and Experience can help us consider more deeply the implications of The United Methodist Church's policies regarding ordination and human sexuality, as well as calls for change and active resistance from annual conferences and Boards of Ordained Ministry.

Scripture

Calling Stories

There are many stories of God calling, ordaining, and sending leaders in the Bible, including Moses encountering the burning bush (Exodus 3:1–4:17), God's consecration of Aaron and the Israelite priesthood (Leviticus 9–10), and Jeremiah's call to prophecy (Jeremiah 1:4-10). One common theme is that those who are called often do not feel worthy. Moses objected to God five times, eventually flatly telling God to choose someone else (Exodus 4:13). Jeremiah objected that he was too young (1:6), and Amos observed that he did not have a prophet's pedigree—he was a shepherd (Amos 7:14-15).

Even though the author of 1 Timothy said that women should not speak in church or have authority over men (1 Timothy 2:11-15), advocates for women's ordination have often pointed out that women were the first people commissioned to spread the good news of Jesus' resurrection (Luke 24:1-11). And in the book of Acts, Peter quotes Joel to highlight diverse people receiving the gift of the Holy Spirit: "Even upon my servants, men and women, I will pour out my Spirit in those days, and they will prophesy" (Acts 2:18).

Apparently, God often calls who God will. Those who support ordination for LGBTQ persons see restrictions on ordination as a restriction on God's Spirit.

Requirements for Clergy

But there are also warning notes about the priesthood in the Scriptures. First Timothy says that church supervisors must be "without fault....They should be faithful to their spouse, sober, modest, and honest" (1 Timothy 3:2). The original Greek actually says, "the husband of one wife" (NASB) instead of "be faithful to their spouse," which fits the author's context. Elsewhere Paul said that he would prefer that "all people were like me"—in other words, unmarried (1 Corinthians 7:7). In any event, the New Testament presents a picture of high standards for those who would lead the church, including integrity and morality in their sexual practices.

In the Old Testament as well as the New, there is a close association with pagan idolatry and loose sexual morals (Numbers 25:1-2, Romans 1:24-25). The holiness of the Israelite priests was supposed to reflect the holiness of God's people. Those who oppose ordination of "self-avowed practicing homosexuals" in The United Methodist Church often see themselves as standing in this tradition of maintaining high standards of holy living with respect to sexuality.

Jesus had hard words for religious leaders who "shut people out of the kingdom of heaven" and "tie together heavy packs that are impossible to carry" (Matthew 23:1-5, 13-15). Advocates for LGBTQ inclusion point out that celibacy is a hard burden placed on gay and lesbian persons that is not likewise placed on straight persons. In other words, preventing LGBTQ clergy from "practicing" their sexuality ties up a heavy burden for them that Jesus would have lamented.

At the same time, Jesus declared that he had come not to abolish the law, but to fulfill it (Matthew 5:17). And his own standards for righteousness exceeded even those of the Pharisees (Matthew 5:20). Those who support the current teachings on ordination would argue that Jesus' warnings against religious leaders' hypocrisy pointed to a higher righteousness and the centrality of love, not a lackadaisical attitude toward morality. The question of how we understand and apply all these passages brings us face to face with our own history and traditions.

Tradition

Requirements for Methodist Preachers

There was a point in our Methodist history where dancing, drinking, and smoking were grounds for punitive action for clergy. The *Book of Discipline* also forbade pastors to perform weddings for previously divorced persons, and as for pastors themselves being divorced—that would have been scandalous.

One Methodist story from the 1760s involves the night Barbara Heck found some of her fellow Irish Methodists playing cards. She disrupted the game, threw the cards into the fire, and then persuaded her cousin, Phillip Embury, to begin preaching at his house.

While many modern Methodists may be amused by old-fashioned restrictions on dancing or card-playing, it does raise questions about whether or not we are as dedicated as those early Methodists. Have we succumbed to the secular notion that our "private" lives have no business being scrutinized in the light of holy living? Our Methodist tradition places a high importance upon holy living, especially among those who would preach and pastor our churches. Those who support the current language in the *Discipline* point out that this includes the ways we live out our sexuality.

It is also worth asking, what does our history and tradition reveal about our understanding of what is important? We do ordain divorced persons now, not because we regard divorce as less tragic, but because we recognize spiritual fruit in the lives of divorced persons who are called to ministry. We have trusted churches and Boards of Ordained Ministry to recognize that fruit, even if Jesus did forbid divorce except in the case of adultery (Matthew 5:31-32). Those who argue for LGBTQ inclusion likewise point to the faithful and fruitful marriages of gay persons as morally equivalent to those of straight persons.

The Ordination of Women

Women were first granted full clergy rights in the Methodist Church in 1956. Until then, many versions of the *Discipline* said

> Our Church does not recognize women as preachers, with authority to occupy the pulpit, to read Holy Scriptures, and to preach, as ministers of the Lord Jesus Christ; nor does it authorize a preacher in charge to invite a woman claiming to be a minister of the Lord Jesus Christ to occupy our pulpits, to expound the Scriptures as a preacher. (¶722, 1930 *Discipline of the Methodist Episcopal Church, South*)

This was despite other leadership roles that had been held by women at various points in Methodist history, including in the early Methodist movement. By contrast, the *Discipline* of the Methodist Church from 1964 says simply, "Women are included in all provisions of the Discipline referring to the ministry" (¶303).

Those who support ordination for LGBTQ persons often compare their situation to that of women in church leadership. Just as The United Methodist Church has come to affirm women's ordination, it ought to begin affirming the ordination of LGBTQ persons. Those who support the current policies in the *Book of Discipline*, however, might point out that it is not one's sexual orientation that is an issue, but one's sexual practices and that one can choose whether or not to engage in same-sex intercourse, but not whether to be a male or a female.

Reason

Calling and Community

In The United Methodist Church's understanding of ordination, a person is *called* by God but that calling is *confirmed* by the community and their clergy peers. In other words, it's an understanding of calling that goes beyond an individual's discernment—the whole church participates in the act of discernment. As the *Discipline* says, "Individuals discern God's call as they relate with God and their communities, and the Church guides and confirms those callings. Calls—and the discernment and confirmation of them—are gifts of the Holy Spirit" (¶301.2). The restriction on ordaining "self-avowed practicing homosexuals" therefore relates to the way in which the church—through the actions of the General Conference—guides and confirms God's calling in an individual's life.

As an act of guidance, this restriction may be the church's way of directing LGBTQ persons toward other forms of ministry and leadership as a fulfillment of their calling, instead of as an ordained clergyperson in The United Methodist Church.

On the other hand, the *Book of Discipline* isn't the only means by which the church community guides and confirms the calling of an individual. The local church, district committees, and Boards of Ordained Ministry also play a role through the whole candidacy process, and as we've already seen, several Boards of Ordained Ministry have decided to ordain LGBTQ persons in spite of the Disciplinary restrictions. It's at these levels that the gifts and evidence of God's grace in an individual are most readily visible to the community. That doesn't mean discernment at local levels should trump the policies of denomination; ideally the various levels would work in harmony and support one another at all stages. But that is not the case at present throughout the Church. In some respects, the debate over whether or not to ordain "self-avowed practicing homosexuals" stems from a tension between these two aspects of the community's guidance and confirmation of God's calling. The General Conference has determined that "self-avowed practicing homosexuals" cannot be ordained, but some local communities have concluded that LGBTQ individuals show evidence of gifts and promise as ordained ministers.

Covenant Questions

Another aspect of the debate concerning ordination includes those clergy who advocate for change through active resistance—such as members of Boards of Ordained Ministry who state that they will not consider a candidate's sexuality in evaluating their fitness for ministry. Clergy members enter into a covenant to uphold the *Book of Discipline*, and they knowingly agree to live by it. "If one does not agree with the *Discipline* on this matter," goes the reasoning, "one should not, in good faith, make a covenant to follow it."

At the same time, part of the *Book of Discipline* that clergy agree to uphold is a means of amending it; the *Book of Discipline* is a living document with a process for making changes. This begs the question of whether we would ever change the *Discipline* at all if we started from the presumption that everyone must agree with all parts before they are ordained. Would we still ordain women if we used the same reasoning? However, the issue does not so much center on a desire to change the *Book of Discipline*, but on a willingness to violate the *Discipline* instead of advocating for change through the prescribed process. It's important to recognize that some believe a willing violation of the *Book of Discipline* is itself an act of advocacy, a way to push for change within the church apart from or in addition to the legislative process of General Conference. The question is whether or not such a means of advocacy is faithful to the clergy covenant—as a form of loyal opposition—or a breaking of it.

Experience

The "experience" aspect of the Wesleyan Quadrilateral is the Christian's experience of salvation, not simply the lived experiences of an individual or group. Those who support the current language in the *Discipline* often highlight this understanding, distinguishing between one's salvation experience and the "experience" of one's sexual orientation. On the other hand, many LGBTQ clergy talk about their own coming out and self-acceptance as an experience of the grace of God and an assurance of their salvation, and they preach from this perspective. They would argue that their salvation and the acceptance of their sexual orientation cannot be separated, but that in coming to accept their sexuality they were assured that God loved them.

It is important in this discussion to realize that many feel the salvation experience of LGBTQ persons in congregations is affirmed—or not—by the presence of LGBTQ pastors in the church. For those who favor inclusion, ordaining LGBTQ persons provides a mirror of the Christian experience of LGBTQ persons in the congregation and one important pathway for them to live out their calling. In a similar way, some women pastors describe coming to The United Methodist Church from denominations that did not ordain women. When they saw women preaching from the pulpit, they realized they could, in fact, pursue their call to ordained ministry.

For those who support the current language in the *Discipline*, ordaining "self-avowed practicing homosexuals" either legitimizes a sinful lifestyle or challenges the biblical witness and the historic teaching of the church. In this view, the salvation experience might include acceptance and peace with one's sexual orientation, but not acceptance of the practice of same-sex intercourse. Celibacy, then, is lifted up as a way for individuals who are same-sex attracted to be responsible stewards of their sexuality. And nothing in the *Discipline* prohibits someone who chooses to be celibate from becoming ordained, regardless of that person's sexual orientation.

Acceptance and Holiness

In many ways, the theological tension between acceptance as we are and the call to a holy way of life is at the heart of the argument over ordination. Which testimony becomes the narrative we preach? Both radical life change and radical acceptance of marginalized people are features of the good news of Jesus Christ. God's boundary-breaking call, the inclusion of women, Samaritans, and Gentiles in Jesus' ministry and the life of the early church, point to the work of God's Spirit in ways that shocked and scandalized religious leaders. The call to the narrow way and the emphasis on accountability and holiness of heart and life also set apart Jesus' ministry as well as the early Methodist movement. How we understand ordination, and the ministry of all baptized Christians, reflects which of these two we emphasize.

Voices

Promises Must Be Kept

When I was ordained in The United Methodist Church, I believed I was entering into a covenant with God, with my fellow clergy, and with the church. The promises I made I regarded to be as sacred as those I made when I married my wife, or when my children were baptized. Included among those promises was that I would abide by the teachings and rules of our *Book of Discipline.*

For more than 200 years, our polity has allowed for profound disagreement and dispute within the context of our system of holy conferencing, imperfect as it is. We have wrestled, wrangled, and argued, but at the end of the day, all sides have been bound to abide by the results of that holy conferencing process, as embodied in our *Book of Discipline.* And there has always been a path for an honorable way to withdraw from the connection for those who felt they could no longer, in good conscience, remain within. From 1784 until just a few years ago, this was universally understood and accepted—this was what we promised.

But now, a significant number of clergy and laity have decided that those promises no longer need to be kept. They are defying our doctrine and discipline, and declaring their intention not to comply with the results of our process of holy conferencing—even while continuing to receive the benefits of remaining within the connection. They have called their actions "civil disobedience," and say that what they are doing is no different than what the civil rights protesters of the 1960s did in defying segregation laws.

But this doesn't wash. The church isn't the government. No one is compelled to join our church as a member, live under our teachings, or be ordained as our clergy. And we have no police force to enforce our discipline. *All that holds us together are the covenantal promises we have made to each other.* When those promises are broken, trust breaks down, and our community cannot long endure.

—Joe Dipaolo, Ordained Elder in The United Methodist Church and member of the Wesleyan Covenant Association
From "Promises Must Be Kept," https://wesleyancovenant. org/2017/04/21/promises-must-be-kept-by-madeline-carrasco-henners/

Will You Accept Us?

There's no sense in denying who I am or God's calling on my life. I am pansexual and gender queer. I am also called to serve as an ordained elder in The UMC.

You may know what it means to be an ordained elder, but have some questions about what it means to be pansexual or gender queer. But, I believe we need to ask the same amount of questions about what it means to be ordained. My gender identity and sexual orientation do not interfere with or change the fact I am called to ordained ministry.

I grew up in the conference from whom I am now seeking ordination. I've personally witnessed the role of a pastor from the perspective of a youth in a suburban, multi-thousand-member congregation. I've served in an urban and a rural small-membership church. I've lived in both the Northeast and the Southeast. They are very different worlds. However, my call never changed. God never abandoned me. Not when I was a youth questioning their sexuality and was called an abomination by someone meant to be my spiritual mentor or when I left home and stopped questioning and came to know myself fully.

I nearly left the church and my calling multiple times. I spent several years away from the church in my early 20s, but found God in a bar, a house of other queer persons, and the freedom of knowing myself. The bar was a small family-owned pub where every regular was treated as a part of the ever-expanding family. We celebrated births and mourned deaths. We shared laughs and stood by one another during hard times. We bought drinks for one another and shared meals. Then, when I went home to the "house of gay," I knew I could be as much of a diva as I needed or watch college football.

I found a love I never knew in a church growing up. I found acceptance.

God creates each of us, loves each of us, calls each of us, and sends each of us.

I am attracted to men, women, trans, and every other category I've encountered. I also don't feel fully defined by either traditional masculine or feminine characteristics. God calls us to unconditional love, which I found in the freedom of knowing myself. I feel free to explore the depths of love as I seek a lifelong partner with whom I may be able to share myself fully.

Yet, I am as much a United Methodist as I am gender queer and pansexual. So, given the current incompatible language of our *Discipline*,

I made a covenant to limit my dating relationships to those of the opposite sex.

Still, the process of changing our *Discipline* is also a part of our *Discipline*, so I remain steadfast in my commitment to The UMC and helping to usher in widespread acceptance in the realm of marriage, ordination, and the full life of the church. My resolve is based not in a fear of rejection, but the hope that future generations of queer United Methodists will not have to experience the hate-filled language of being labeled as incompatible or an abomination for seeking to love and be loved.

Queer children and youth will only continue to find temporary residence in our congregations until our language changes. As stewards of their spiritual development, I implore our church to consider how they are being shaped into mature, self-sufficient, adult Christians. If you tell a child they are incompatible or an abomination, that is all they will ever see themselves as in your presence.

So, I seek ordination, not as someone afraid to speak, but as someone who hopes to speak for myself and with others in places we are not welcome but go anyway. God creates, loves, calls, and sends us.

Will you accept us?

—A Queer Provisional Elder

Chapter 4

WHERE ARE WE NOW?

By Alex Joyner

The In-Between Time

United Methodists are among the most broadly distributed Christian denominations and have traditionally represented a wide diversity of perspectives. In recent years, as debates and movements within American culture over human sexuality have led to sweeping changes in the legal rights of LGBTQ persons, including the right to marry, United Methodists have been examining their own beliefs and practices in light of God's call to personal holiness and the beloved community. As this book has shown, just like the country at large, United Methodists in the United States have ended up in different places.

Along with the particular questions about how the Bible, tradition, experience, and reason speak to human sexuality, there has been another yearning within the denomination—a desire for unity. "Look how good and pleasing it is when families live together as one!" Psalm 133:1 declares. In the United Methodist Communion liturgy, the words of the Great Thanksgiving invoke the Holy Spirit to "make us one with Christ, one with each other, and one in ministry to all the world."[1] Many United Methodists have been longing for a new expression of church that allows for this sense of one-ness and connection.

In this in-between time, marked by the close of the 2016 General Conference and the anticipation of a special General Conference in early 2019, some recent events have highlighted the ongoing tensions over sexuality questions. But we have also seen the early work of a commission that has been formed with a grand purpose: to discern a way forward, not just for the areas of division, but for the church as a whole.

The Commission on a Way Forward Emerges from the 2016 General Conference

In Portland, Oregon, at the May 2016 General Conference, the quadrennial global gathering of United Methodists, there were signs of great division. During the first week, when much of the conference work was in legislative committees, resolutions related to sexuality were fiercely debated. Supporters of greater inclusion for LGBTQ persons lined walkways in silent protest and interested persons lingered outside the doorways of the committee meetings. Tensions remained high as the General Conference headed into its second week, when resolutions would head to the full plenary session on the conference floor. Talk of schism was in the air.

During the floor debate, the General Conference called upon the bishops to take leadership in moving the church forward. "We are in a stuck place at this General Conference.... I'm pleading with you. Please help us," said the Rev. Adam Hamilton, pastor of the Church of the Resurrection in Kansas City.[2]

---

1 "A Service of Word and Table II," *The United Methodist Hymnal* (Nashville, The United Methoidst Publishing House, 1989), 14.

2 Kathy Gilbert and Sam Hodges, "Conference pleads with bishops for leadership," United Methodist News Service, May 17, 2016, accessed July 27, 2017, http://www.umc.org/news-and-media/conference-pleads-with-bishops-for-leadership, referred to hereafter as GC 17 May 2016.

The next day, Bishop Bruce Ough, president of the Council of Bishops, said, "We accept our role as spiritual leaders to lead The United Methodist Church in a 'pause for prayer'—to step back from attempts at legislative solutions and to intentionally seek God's will for the future."[3] The Council proposed suspending any votes on human sexuality during the 2016 General Conference and establishing a commission to review all of the language related to human sexuality in the *Book of Discipline* and possibly to recommend revisions to the bishops.

The proposal, which was narrowly approved, included the possibility for the bishops to call a special session of the General Conference prior to 2020, (when the next General Conference had been scheduled to meet). The purpose of such a special session would be to act on a report from the Council of Bishops based on legislation that might emerge from this new Commission on a Way Forward. The Commission, made up of thirty-two persons drawn from all parts of the church and with varied perspectives on the question of human sexuality, began meeting in January 2017.

A special General Conference has been scheduled for February 23–26, 2019, in St. Louis, Missouri. While each annual conference may elect new delegates to the 2019 General Conference, it is expected that most conferences will send the same delegation that attended the 2016 gathering.

The Election and Consecration of Karen Oliveto

The bishops' call at General Conference for a "pause for prayer…to intentionally seek God's will for the future," was interpreted by many as a sign that the status quo with regard to sexuality decisions would remain in effect until a called General Conference. The language of the *Book of Discipline* had not changed, but new events challenged that presumed equilibrium. One of them was the election of Karen Oliveto as a bishop in the Western Jurisdiction.

---

3 Heather Hahn and Sam Hodges, "GC2016 puts hold on sexuality debate," United Methodist News Service, May 18, 2016, accessed July 27, 2017, www.umc.org/news-and-media/bishops-ask-for-hold-on-sexuality-debate

As jurisdictional conferences in the United States met to elect bishops two months after the 2016 General Conference, three of those nominated were openly gay. One of them, the Rev. Karen Oliveto, was the accomplished senior pastor of historic Glide Memorial UMC in San Francisco in the California-Nevada Conference. She was also married to another woman and open about her same-sex orientation.

In offering herself for the episcopacy, Rev. Oliveto said, "I am very supportive of the Bishop's Way Forward…I believe that what this commission will discover is that while matters of human sexuality are the symptom, the dis-ease within our denomination is cultural and theological and it is impacting our ability to create disciples of Jesus Christ for the transformation of the world. Unfortunately, LGBTQ persons have paid a harsh price for our neglect in speaking the truth about our denomination."[4]

On July 15, 2016, Rev. Oliveto was elected bishop by members of Western Jurisdictional Conference after other candidates dropped out in her favor. The election was celebrated by Western Jurisdiction bishops who saw it as a recognition of Oliveto's manifest gifts for the office. Bishop Grant Hagiya told United Methodist News Service (UMNS), "We understand there may be some political implications, but in our mind this was the best person. It was not a question of (sexual) orientation, it was a question of who was the best spiritual leader."[5]

The South Central Jurisdiction was still meeting at the time and, on a 109–84 vote, they petitioned the Judicial Council for a ruling on the eligibility of an openly gay person to serve as a bishop. Some saw the election of Bishop Oliveto as a betrayal of the spirit of the General Conference's action in creating a Commission. The Rev. Thomas

---

4 Kathy L. Gilbert, "3 gay pastors among nominees for bishop," United Methodist News Service, June 29, 2016, accessed July 27, 2017, www.umc.org/news-and-media/3-gay-pastors-among-nominees-for-bishop

5 Kathy L. Gilbert, "Married lesbian consecrated United Methodist bishop," United Methodist News Service, July 16, 2016, accessed July 27, 2017, http://www.umc.org/news-and-media/married-lesbian-consecrated-united-methodist-bishop

Lambrecht told United Methodist News Services, "It is regrettable that we have reached the point of such open defiance of the decisions made in good faith by our global United Methodist Church."[6] Lambrecht is the vice president and general manager of Good News, an organization that supports retaining current language in the *Book of Discipline.*

The Judicial Council ruling on Oliveto's consecration finally came on April 28, 2017. The Council found that the consecration of a gay bishop was a violation of church law, but it did not overturn Oliveto's status as a bishop. However, in the ruling, the Council declared that a clergy person in a same-sex marriage was in violation of the *Book of Discipline's* provision that "self-avowed practicing homosexuals are not to be certified as candidates, ordained as ministers, or appointed to serve in The United Methodist Church" (¶304.3).

Therefore, the Judicial Council reasoned, Rev. Oliveto's ministerial status should be reviewed by the Western Jurisdiction through its normal due process. The Council of Bishops might also be asked to intervene if that review did not take place. The status of that review was ongoing at the time of this writing and Bishop Oliveto continues to serve as the episcopal leader of the Mountain Sky Area based in Denver.

The Wesleyan Covenant Association

Meanwhile, another movement has begun energizing evangelicals within The United Methodist Church. Organizers of the Wesleyan Covenant Association (WCA) announced plans in the summer of 2016 to hold an inaugural gathering in Chicago. A number of prominent evangelical voices in the church, including the Rev. Maxie Dunnam, Rev. Jeff Greenway, and Rev. Madeline Carrasco Henners, announced their support for the WCA, as did the leadership of the Confessing Movement, an existing evangelical caucus within The UMC.

---

6 Gilbert, "3 gay pastors among nominees for bishop."

The WCA has presented itself as a home for United Methodists who feel that the debate over human sexuality issues is overwhelming the mission of the church and distracting from Wesleyan essentials. The Chicago gathering in October 2016 drew over 1,700 people and adopted a definition of the association as a "coalition of congregations, clergy, and laity from across The United Methodist Church, committed to promoting ministry that combines a high view of Scripture, Wesleyan vitality, orthodox theology, and Holy Spirit empowerment."[7]

While the WCA statement covers many areas of belief, in an accompanying statement on the Commission on a Way Forward, the WCA makes clear that the current restrictions on ordination of gay clergy and same-sex marriage are non-negotiable. "If the commission determines no...[unity] plan is possible," the statement says, "then we believe it should prepare a plan of separation that honors the consciences of all the people of the church and allows them to go forward in peace and good will."[8]

"My focus is going to be on where we're going as a church and where we're going as the Wesleyan Covenant Association," the Rev. Keith Boyette said soon after his election as the first president of the WCA in April 2017.[9]

But others have seen the WCA as a prelude to a schism: a network of conservative churches building a rival denominational structure that would enable a split. In May 2017, The Orchard, a prominent, large-membership church in Tupelo, Mississippi, with strong evangelical leadership, broke away from The United Methodist Church. When it was announced that the senior pastor of the church, Dr. Bryan Collier, would remain on the governing board of the WCA, it seemed to some to confirm their suspicion that the WCA was preparing for a separation.

---

7 "Statements/Beliefs," Wesleyan Covenant Association, https://wesleyancovenant.org/wca-statements-and-beliefs/

8 Ibid.

9 Heather Hahn, "Evangelical group plans for what's next," United Methodist News Service, May 1, 2017, accessed July 27, 2017, http://www.umc.org/news-and-media/evangelical-group-plans-for-whats-next

In responding to The Orchard's decision, the WCA leadership stated, "Whatever the future holds, we know that we want to face it together…. The Wesleyan Covenant Association is committed to being a landing place for persons and congregations who desire to be part of a global expression of vibrant, orthodox, Wesleyan Christianity as we live into what is next."[10]

African Responses

The ongoing discussions over human sexuality within The United Methodist Church come as the denomination has truly become a global church. Particularly in Africa, the church has been growing rapidly, and that growth was reflected in the composition of the 2016 General Conference. African delegates made up over thirty percent of the eight hundred sixty-four delegates, and they were very visible and vocal. This is in contrast to the percentage of US delegates, which has been declining. Perhaps as soon as the 2020 General Conference, US delegates will constitute less than half of the body.

The conversation about sexuality in Africa and other parts of the world takes place in a cultural context much different from that of the United States. "In African culture it is 'taboo' to speak about sexuality," Kasap Owan Tshibang, a Congolese delegate, told the 2004 General Conference. "We do not want to be caught up in the issue."[11]

Some African United Methodist leaders have seen the continuing debate over sexuality in the denomination as a challenge to their biblical understanding and to their notion of the connection. "Those violating the Bible and the *Book of Discipline* of The UMC are saying to the global UMC community that they are taking their exit

---

10 "Statements/Beliefs," Wesleyan Covenant Association.

11 Ervin Dyer, "United Methodists reaffirm line on gays," *Pittsburgh Post-Gazette*, May 5, 2004, accessed July 27, 2017, http://www.post-gazette.com/news/nation/2004/05/05/United-Method-ists-reaffirm-line-on-gays/stories/200405050212

and transferring their loyalty somewhere else," the Rev. Jerry Kulah, dean of Gbarnga School of Theology in Liberia, said in a UMNS report.[12]

A Methodist Middle

The landscape of the discussion over human sexuality has been largely defined by those who favor full inclusion of LGBTQ persons and those who see ordination of gay clergy and same-sex marriage as an abandonment of core biblical teachings. But there is also a concerted effort to find middle ground between these two poles.

Some of the strongest supporters of the Commission on a Way Forward have described themselves as centrists. They gathered in May 2017 at a conference entitled, "To Serve the Present Age," to share their hopes for the denomination and to bolster their belief that a broad 'Methodist middle' exists.[13]

In trying to describe the centrist position, the Rev. Tom Berlin, who is also a member of the Commission on a Way Forward, outlines four categories (which he credits to Thomas Lambrecht), which apply to most United Methodists in the United States on the questions of ordination and marriage:

- On one end are **Traditionalist Non-compatibilists**. This is a group for whom the traditional standards of The UMC on marriage and ordination are so important that they could not accept a denomination in which parts of the church operated with different standards. For people in this group, upholding the current restrictions on ordination and marriage is a matter of integrity and fidelity to the Scriptures.

---

12 Gilbert, "Married lesbian consecrated United Methodist bishop."

13 Kathy L. Gilbert, "'Methodist Middle' Committed to Living Together," United Methodist News Service, May 18, 2017, accessed July 27, 2017, http://um-insight.net/in-the-church/a-way-forward/'methodist-middle'-committed-to-living-together/

- The next group Berlin describes as **Traditionalist Compatibilists**. Persons in this group generally hold the same traditional view on these questions, but they are willing to accept a diversity of beliefs and practices on ordination and marriage within the larger church. A denomination in which some accepted same-gender marriage and LGBTQ ordination—but they themselves were not required to — would be acceptable to them.

- **Progressive Compatibilists** are also content with a denomination that has room for different viewpoints, though their own beliefs lead them to favor ordination of gay clergy and celebration of same-gender marriage. A denomination in which some clergy, local churches, or annual conferences did not have that same belief is acceptable to them.

- **Progressive Non-compatibilists**, on the other hand, feel that the full inclusion of LGBTQ persons is a matter of justice and faithfulness to Jesus' model of acceptance of all persons. Their goal is a denomination that, in all its expressions, practices and affirms ordination and marriage of gay persons.[14]

Berlin has estimated that the two compatibilist groupings represent about seventy percent of US United Methodists. If this center were freed from the burden of endless debates over human sexuality, Berlin says, it might be able to address more critical issues like church vitality and making disciples of Jesus Christ for the transformation of the world.[15]

It's important to note that others have a different view of the traditional, progressive, and centrist perspectives. Chris Ritter, a self-described "Traditionalist Incompatibilist," believes that most centrists are in fact "Progressive Compatibilists," and that "Traditionalist

---

14 Tom Berlin, "Getting to Church Vitality," June 21, 2016, accessed July 27, 2017, http:// revtomberlin.com/church-vitality/#sthash.TPHqmXna.dpbs

15 Ibid.

Compatibilists" are relatively rare. In his view, what Berlin and others describe as the middle ground is actually closer to the progressive perspective than to the traditional. And, he says, the "Traditionalist Non-compatibilists" represent the largest and most diverse group of United Methodists.[16]

These differing understandings of the landscape of the human sexuality debate highlight how ambiguous things presently are, and how difficult it is to describe the current reality or make predictions about the future of the denomination.

"It's Time to Stop Destroying the Couch"

Berlin's outline of the four positions has come to be known as "the sugar packet" model because he has illustrated it using restaurant-sized sugar packets. In the illustration, each position has its own packet and they are contained within a larger box that represents the covenantal relationship of the *Book of Discipline* that holds United Methodists together. As actions are taken that are seen by some as "impinging on their conscience," as Berlin has described it (such as Boards of Ordained Ministry declaring that they will no longer consider a person's sexual orientation in their ordination process or church trials brought against clergy who perform marriage rites for same-sex couples), some persons start to drift away from the church. This is visually represented in Berlin's illustration by tears in the sugar packets that leave scattered grains of sugar. The overall effect is to suggest that the stability of all four groups is compromised by the current environment of repeated conflict over human sexuality issues.[17]

At a presentation to the Virginia Annual Conference in 2017, Berlin compared his experience of recent General Conferences to the time he

---

16 Chris Ritter, "Why are 'Traditional Compatibilists' So Hard to Find?," May 10, 2017, accessed July 28, 2017, https://wesleyancovenant.org/2017/05/10/why-are-traditionalist-compatiblists-so-hard-to-find-by-chris-ritter/.

17 Berlin, "Getting to Church Vitality"

came home to find that the family dog had torn apart the couch. The dog seemed to look at him in bewilderment about how such a mess could have happened and, of course, didn't have words to describe his part in it. Berlin made the connection to how he feels about the sometimes painful parliamentary tactics of groups and speakers at General Conference. "It's time to stop destroying the couch while calling it holy conferencing," Berlin said.

This is not just an appeal for greater civility or a call to diminish the need for discussion about deeply held values, but it is an effort to focus the discussion on the nature of the connection that binds United Methodists together. In theological language, *ecclesiology* is the name given to discussions about what we believe about the church.

Berlin's comments imply that the struggle may really be about finding a new way to be church. At the same presentation in 2017, he advocated "walking together loosely," which is "a shift from seeking to come to agreement.... It allows us to concentrate on mission objectives." But such a shift would entail reconceiving the relationships of the connection—a new ecclesiology.

An emphasis on the church's missional priority is shared even by those who dispute Berlin's characterization of the centrist perspective. Those traditionalists who want to end the sexuality debate by enforcing the *Book of Discipline* more strictly—or by separating from the church—seek primarily to be freed from the sexuality debate to focus on making disciples of Jesus Christ with a commitment to Christian orthodoxy and Wesleyan holiness. Likewise, those who are progressive push for change, even violate the *Book of Discipline*, because justice for LGBTQ persons is for them a missional priority. All perspectives share an understanding of the status quo in the human sexuality debate as an obstacle to the Church's mission. Where they differ is on the best way to move forward, and what changes to our ecclesiology need to be made.

A Short History of United Methodist Polity

Methodists have always been pragmatic about church structure. The early conferences that led, in 1784, to the formation of the Methodist Episcopal Church (a predecessor to today's United Methodist Church) debated fiercely over questions of polity, or church structure. In the wake of the American Revolution, American Methodists had to consider what authority would look like in a church that was formally separated from the Anglican Church from which it had grown and to some degree from its former leader, John Wesley.

The resulting church adopted a polity that combined the traditional office of episcopal leaders, or bishops (hence Episcopal), with a conference structure that shared the democratic ideals of the emerging American nation. The modern United Methodist Church has inherited this hybrid structure which places most of its legislative authority in a representative body (the General Conference) of clergy and laity and pairs it with a Council of Bishops which has tremendous responsibility through administration, organization of annual conferences, and clergy supervision and appointment.

While some matters have been delegated to the regional central conferences, jurisdictional conferences, and annual conferences, authoritative decisions about ordination and marriage of gay persons have always been made by the General Conference. The present divisions on these questions have led some to wonder if that structure is still adequate.

Should there be a smaller *Book of Discipline* that allows for more decisions to be made on the regional or even local church level? Given that conversations on sexuality are very different in, say, Africa, the Philippines, and the United States, this has some appeal. But differing positions are contained within annual conferences in the United States and within individual congregations. Some feel that regional or local church options would just move the divisions from the General Conference to these levels. And while such options would be acceptable to "centrists," as Berlin's sugar packets demonstration showed, they would not be acceptable to those who want the whole denomination to be of one mind, whether progressive or traditional.

Amicable Separation

If loosening the present United Methodist connection doesn't turn out to be a viable option—for any number of reasons—the result may be a separation within the denomination. In fact, there are some who think this is the best option for moving forward. In such a view, the rifts within The United Methodist Church are too great to allow us to remain together; there is already insurmountable distance between the theological commitments of traditionalists and progressives. Separation, the reasoning goes, is the only way to allow both sides to flourish on their own terms.

Such a separation would not be easy. Our denominational structure binds our annual conferences and churches together in practical, material ways, which include things like ownership of church property and pension liability for retired clergy. If a local church or an annual conference were to withdraw from the denomination, these matters would have to be resolved, and doing so could result in legal battles, financial expenditures, and damaged relationships. And there would be an impact on our denomination-wide agencies and initiatives, since every church and annual conference contributes to them through their apportionment payments. All of these consequences would multiply if a large number of churches and annual conferences decided to split away.

Recognizing these difficulties, some have called for a plan of "amicable separation" that would reduce practical obstacles, minimize hostility, and allow parties who cannot remain together to part ways in peace. Like Paul and Barnabas who went their separate ways in Acts, each party could remain true to their commitment and calling unhindered (Acts 15:36-41).

A separation could take shape in several different ways. Some scenarios involve one or more groups breaking away from the current United Methodist Church. To return to Berlin's sugar packets model, the "Non-compatibilists"—either progressives, traditionalists, or both—could leave the denomination. Those who remain would retain the United Methodist name and control of denomination-wide agencies, while making concessions that would ease the departure of those who choose to leave. Churches or conferences that leave would then be free to form a new denomination—or join another existing denomination, or simply remain independent. A separation along these lines could largely be accomplished with the existing policies of The United Methodist Church. It's unclear, however, whether such a separation would truly resolve—or merely postpone or prolong—the debate regarding human sexuality.

Other scenarios might involve replacing The United Methodist Church with two or three new denominations, aligned with traditionalist, progressive, and centrist views. These new denominations would each have an independent structure, which would allow them to remain true to their theological commitments. They could retain some connection to one another through communion relationships, partnerships in service and mission, and shared resources. Under our current policies, a separation like this would require amendments to our constitution (¶1–61 in the *Book of Discipline*), meaning it couldn't be accomplished until at least 2020, since any amendments to the constitution have to be ratified by at least two-thirds of all the annual conferences after they are passed by the General Conference.

It's important to bear in mind that in any of the above scenarios, separation would not be solely based on views of human sexuality, same-gender marriage, and the ordination of LGBTQ persons. Rather, the differing views of progressives and traditionalists stem from other, more fundamental differences—including the ways we interpret Scripture, the sources of authority for our theology, and the ways we approach mission and outreach. Those who call for amicable separation point out that the opposing views regarding human sexuality are only the most visible aspect of the divisions that exist.

Despite these ongoing tensions, some find hope in the 2016 General Conference action which resulted in the bishops forming a Commission on a Way Forward. The request from the General Conference for the bishops to provide leadership felt like a new approach. Several observed at the time that they couldn't recall the Conference directly asking for the bishops' guidance in this way.

The Commission on a Way Forward, committed to extended, prayerful deliberation, will report its findings to the Council of Bishops, and the General Conference will act on the bishops' recommendations in the special session in 2019. Until that time, the Commission has requested that United Methodists pray for them and their work.

A Time for Conversation and New Community

So, what to do with this in-between time? Rather than "waiting on the world to change" (or the church), to borrow a phrase from John Mayer, maybe we could begin to model the church we hope to be.

In their book *Longing for Spring: A New Vision for Wesleyan Community*, United Methodist authors Elaine Heath and Scott Kisker talk about the opportunity this age presents for reclaiming the heart of the Wesleyan and Christian message. "We are in a full-blown institutional crisis. Is this a bad thing? [We] don't think so," they say.[18] Though they refer specifically to the realities of declining attendance and participation in churches, their insight that crisis leads to opportunity is applicable here as well. "Today there are plenty of seekers looking for a model for creating down-to-earth yet spiritual expressions of community. What is needed are multiple examples of how to do it."[19]

The Rev. Tom Berlin urges United Methodists to model new community through the practice of talking to one another. "What leaders

---

18 Elaine Heath and Scott T. Kisker, *Longing for Spring: A New Vision for Wesleyan Community*, (Eugene, OR, Cascade Books, 2010), 9.

19 Ibid., 20..

don't do is avoid conversation," he said at the Virginia Annual Conference in 2017. He initiated conversations around these sexuality questions in Floris UMC, the diverse church in northern Virginia where he serves. "The church has not fallen in," he affirmed.

Full inclusion of LGBTQ persons and diversity of biblical interpretation are important to explore. But we may not be able to go far in the conversation unless we first have spirits formed by Christian community and the disciplines of that community. Without that soil to grow in, our debates will look suspiciously like those that dominate our divided nation.

Ephesians 2:11-22 offers, as a way to think about unity, the person of Christ. Verse 14 says, "Christ is our peace. He made both Jews and Gentiles into one group. With his body, he broke down the barrier of hatred that divided us." One measure of how we are doing in this time is how close we are to that peace.

Voices

The Gift I've Been Given

As John Donne so famously said, no man is an island. We don't exist in a vacuum, and when one identifies oneself as gay or lesbian, it creates a circle of pain. When I finally recognized myself as a lesbian, I knew that I was asking those closest to me, especially my family, to make big sacrifices in order to support me. I agonized seeing the ones I love hurting so much because of me.

Throughout the upheaval I prayed, and I felt uplifted by the sense that I was still in the palm of God's hand. I was still loved. God was still in control and directing me. I felt guilt over the pain I was causing others, but I sensed God was forgiving me and working in my life and the lives of my loved ones.

As I was finding and identifying myself as a homosexual person, I knew with certainty that this was not in itself a sin. I came to regard it as a gift. I did not know where this new road would take me, but I sensed it was where I belonged, that it was my destiny.

I deeply love my life partner. The Bible in the First Letter of John teaches that we love because God first loved us. God is love. Love is god manifested in human relationships. I believe when two people love each other deeply, spiritually, wholly, it is a love from God, of God, sanctified by God.

I often think with amazement at the genius of God the Creator and at the delight God must have expressed when he/she came up with another really great idea. Take rainbows, for example. Now who would have ever thought that up? Or fireflies? Or *snow*? I can imagine God the Creator chuckling and thinking, "The kids will really *love* this."

Why is it so difficult for us to believe that a God who wants to make ten thousand different varieties of trees and millions of different species and is creative enough to want every snowflake different—that that God couldn't create and bless more than one type of human sexual expression?

There is a popular saying, "God don't make junk." On a profound level, I believe that to be true. In Genesis, God declared *all* that God made to be good. That certainly includes all of God's children.

It is we, not God, who label God's children 'deviant' and call them 'queer.' Doesn't it seem arrogant that we should so judge God's creation? God's own children? Are left-handed people deviant? Are short people deviant? What about blue-eyed people, are they deviant? People are brown and yellow and black and white and gay and straight and bisexual and transgender. Are all of us not another expression of God's love for uniqueness in his/her creatures?

Loving and being loved is not a sin, it is a gift of grace. That gift is often provided to a man and a woman and sometimes also to persons of the same sex. We are very blessed if we find our soul mate. Our sexual orientation is part of our package. It is part of our uniqueness. I am happy with the gift I have been given.

—Nancy A. Thomason

From *Journeying Toward Reconciliation: Personal Stories of Faith, Sexuality, and the Church* (Waynesville, NC: First United Methodist Church of Waynesville, CreateSpace Independent Publishing Platform, 2015), 26–27.

The Global UMC and Our Common World

As leaders of the church in Africa, we call upon all United Methodists, Bishops, clergy and Laity to an unreserved commitment to the Holy Bible as the primary authority for faith and practice in the church. We call upon all members throughout the connection to adopt practices consistent with the teachings of the Holy Scriptures. We submit to the teachings of Scripture that God designed marriage to be between man and woman, and the procreation of children is a blessing from God (Gen. 2:24-25; Psalm 127:3-5). Scripture also teaches that all persons are sexual beings, whether or not they are married. However, sexual relations are affirmed only within the covenant bond of a faithful monogamous, heterosexual marriage, and not within same-sex unions or polygamy. The Christian marriage covenant is holy, sacred, and consecrated by God and is expressed in shared fidelity between one man and one woman for life. In this vein, we denounce all forms of sexual exploitation, including fornication, adultery, sexual commercialization, slavery, abuse, polygamy, etc.

One of the functions of the Bishops of the church is to "maintain the unity of the church". As leaders of the church, we believe that there are far more important issues that unite us than issues of sexual orientation. As a church, we are called to be in solidarity with people who suffer as a result of unjust political systems, wars, famine, poverty, natural disasters, diseases, illiteracy, etc. We believe that we can be united around these issues rather than allow ourselves to be ripped apart by issues of sexual orientation.

—Africa College of Bishops

From "A Statement on the State of Global UMC and Our Common World," September 11, 2015.

LEADER GUIDE

GUIDANCE FOR GROUP LEADERS

The topic you will discuss in this book is by its nature controversial, and for many people it prompts strong emotions. In preparation for leading this class, you might find it useful to develop ground rules for discussion and review them with your group before you start. Consider posting these rules in a visible place so you can refer back to them should the conversation become heated.

Do not hesitate to stop discussions if you find that one or more participants seems agitated, angry, or hurt. You can then lead a brief time of prayer for the group, or simply ask participants to spend a few moments in silence. Review your ground rules again before resuming the discussion.

You might have a group where participants are all in agreement on the issues being discussed. In this case, it's even more important to avoid an "us vs. them" mentality or inflammatory language. Otherwise, your group will not learn anything new or grow in understanding. As the leader, it is your role to make sure all viewpoints are presented fully and fairly. Consider meditating on John 13:35 before you lead the class ("This is how everyone will know that you are my disciples, when you love each other.")

The following is an example of discussion rules, which you can use as they appear or modify to fit your needs:

- Listen respectfully, without interrupting.

- Listen actively and with an ear to understanding others' views. (Don't just think about what you are going to say while someone else is talking.)

- Criticize ideas, not individuals.

- Commit to learning, not debating. Comment in order to share information, not to persuade.

- Avoid blame, speculation, and inflammatory language.

- Allow everyone the chance to speak.

- Avoid assumptions about any member of the class or generalizations about social groups. Do not ask individuals to speak for their (perceived) social group.

(From the Center for Research on Learning and Teaching, University of Michigan)[1]

Helpful Resources and Links

At each of your group meetings, have some hard copies of *The Book of Discipline of The United Methodist Church, 2016* and *The Book of Resolutions of The United Methodist Church, 2016* available for the class to see and reference. Check in your church library to find copies of these books, or consult your pastor about where you might find them in your church. Also have some Bibles available in a variety of translations. Be aware that some participants may prefer using digital Bible apps on their smartphones.

Digital versions of the *Book of Discipline* and the *Book of Resolutions* can be found at this link: https://www.cokesbury.com/forms/DynamicContent.aspx?id=87&pageid=920

Additional information about John Wesley's teachings can be found at this link: http://www.umc.org/what-we-believe/our-wesleyan-heritage

For news about recent events in The United Methodist Church, check out United Methodist News Service (UMNS) at this link: http://www.umc.org/news-and-media/united-methodist-news

---

1 http://www.crlt.umich.edu/publinks/generalguidelines - rules

Chapter 1

IS THE PRACTICE OF HOMOSEXUALITY INCOMPATIBLE WITH CHRISTIAN TEACHING?

Create Your Own Teaching Plan

Keeping in mind your group members and your group time, choose from among the OPEN, EXPLORE, and CLOSE activities to plan this session.

OPEN the Session

Pray Together

Open the session with the following prayer:

Loving God, you call us to unity, but we are inclined to division. We live in a conflict-ridden world that separates friends, families, churches, and nations. The world models extreme opinions and closed ears. You call us to be set apart, to be holy, to be different from the world. Our self-centered nature makes it hard for us to truly hear and understand perspectives that differ from our own. We call upon your Holy Spirit to open our hearts as we discuss this topic today; in Christ's name. Amen.

Introduce the Topic

Ask participants: What concerns do you have as we begin this study on *Human Sexuality and The United Methodist Church*? What does the term "living faithfully" mean to you? Can you think of an issue—other than human sexuality—on which you held a strong belief at one time, but then changed your view or came to appreciate the other perspective? If you feel comfortable, share what that experience was like and what you learned from it.

Ground Rules

Invite a group member to read the ground rules for discussing with one another on pages 86–87, then ask if any modifications would be useful for your group. Ensure that the group doesn't spend too much time on this. Invite each person to commit to following these ground rules during your discussions together.

EXPLORE the Topic

Discuss Controversy as Opportunity

Read or review the opening paragraphs of chapter one and the first section of it, "Controversy as Opportunity." Ask: What do you hope to learn from this study? Is this an "urgent topic of concern" for you? Why or why not? Do you feel God calling you to grow in your listening skills? Explain your answer.

Invite the group to recall the instances of controversy in the early church, and to name any others that they might be aware of. Ask: What are some examples of controversial issues the modern church has to deal with, outside of sexuality? Have you been a part of a church that had to deal with a conflict on a particular issue? What was it and how was it resolved?

Ask: What resources do United Methodists look to for Christian teaching? What sources do you consult as an individual? What resources do we all have as common sources of authority? How do our attitudes toward these sources differ, and why?

Learn about the *Book of Discipline*

After reviewing the "History and Purpose" of the *Book of Discipline* section, ask: When was the last time you held a United Methodist *Book of Discipline* in your hands? Have you ever? How familiar are you with its contents? What did you learn from this section?

Review "Statements on Human Sexuality" and "Timeline of Statements," then ask: Which, if any, of these statements from the *Book of Discipline* are you already familiar with? Which ones surprised you? What did you learn from this section? What questions do you still have?

If anyone in your class attended the 2016 General Conference, or followed closely the events at this session, ask them to give a brief summary of what happened there.

Review Wesleyan Theology

After reading "Grace and Holiness," ask participants to share their thoughts on John Wesley's theology. If there is time, review all twenty-two of the questions with which Wesley and the others would examine their lives. The questions can be found at: https://www.umc-discipleship.org/resources/everyday-disciples-john-wesleys-22-questions

Ask: What are your thoughts on these questions? Would you be willing to ask these questions of yourself every day?

Read the paragraphs under "Wesleyan Quadrilateral" and "How is the Wesleyan Quadrilateral being used in the debate over homosexuality." Then ask: How have you used the Wesleyan Quadrilateral in your own theological reflections? How does this method help you understand the character of God better? How does it help you understand God's eternal purpose better? Is this tool useful for the debate over homosexuality? Why or why not?

Consider Biblical Interpretations

Review the section "Differing Interpretations." Ask: Do you believe Christians should all interpret Scripture in the same way? Why or why not?

Review the Bible passages listed under "Differing Interpretations." If there is time, read the full passage of the verses cited out loud. State: It's likely we bring different views to these passages. As we discuss them, let us remember our ground rules for discussions.

For each passage, ask: How is God leading you to interpret this passage? Do you find it relevant for today? Why or why not?

Ask if any participants are willing to summarize in their own words the views that traditionalists and progressives might have on these passages. Then ask: Are there other interpretations besides these views? Give examples.

You can also ask participants to review 2 Corinthians 5:19 and Luke 10:27, which were referenced in the Wesleyan Quadrilateral section. Ask: What are your thoughts on these verses? What passages in Scripture, for you, best reflect the "larger biblical witness" about human sexuality?

CLOSE the Session

Reflection

Read aloud "Conclusion" then state: Take a moment to consider how this discussion affected you today. Did it make you angry? Did it give you comfort? Where have you been challenged in your faith? What spiritual practices do you need to add to your walk with Christ? In what ways can differing views be a gift to Christ's church?

Invite participants to write down their answers, or simply reflect on them quietly.

Also encourage participants to engage in the following action during the next week, then report back on their interactions at the beginning of your next meeting:

Seek out someone in your life whom you know has a different view on homosexuality than you do. Ask them how they arrived at their belief. Ask them how they think their belief has been misunderstood. The goal is to just listen and ask questions, not engage in a debate. Pray for this person throughout your week.

Pray Together

Close with the following prayer:

God of Creation, your love for us is vast and abundant. We see that radical love in the life, death, and resurrection of Christ. Jesus was never afraid to ask questions, or to answer a question with another question. He taught us to seek first the kingdom of God, not certainty. Help us to follow Christ's example. We pray for those whose lives have been harmed or otherwise affected by The United Methodist Church's teachings on human sexuality. We also pray for all church leaders— laity, clergy, and bishops—who must make decisions on the future of The United Methodist Church. Lift their spirits. Give them hearts of compassion and minds of wisdom. And most importantly, help us all to abide in you; in Christ's name. Amen.

Chapter 2

IS SAME-GENDER MARRIAGE COMPATIBLE WITH CHRISTIAN TEACHING?

Create Your Own Teaching Plan

Keeping in mind your group members and your group time, choose from among the OPEN, EXPLORE, and CLOSE activities to plan this session.

OPEN the Session

Pray Together

Use the following prayer to open your time together, or offer a prayer of your own choosing:

God who is our hope, as we gather together today, each of us brings different feelings and experiences with us. As we explore the some-times contentiousness subject of marriage, guide our hearts and our minds. Help us to listen for where you are leading your church. May your Spirit help us to understand our sisters and brothers, even those we may deeply disagree with. Open us to new understanding and a deeper love for all our neighbors. Amen.

Provide Guidance about Communication

Before beginning today's session, briefly review the ground rules for conversing together on pages 86–87 (or as modified by your group at your previous session). Encourage all who are participating, in the words of

Bishop Kenneth Carter, to "begin with an intention of seeing the best in each other."[2]

EXPLORE the Topic

Create a Timeline

Refer to the section of this chapter titled "Current *Book of Discipline* Statements Related to Marriage." See also the section "Statements on Human Sexuality" in chapter one. As needed, take a moment to review what General Conference is, as well as what the *Book of Discipline* is. Using a large piece of paper or a markerboard, make a timeline of statements that have been passed by General Conferences related to homosexuality and same-gender marriage. Invite group members to identify when on the timeline they became part of The United Methodist Church. Ask: Do you recall discussion of any of these decisions that were made at the time? Do you feel like these decisions have had an impact on ministry taking place in your local church? In what ways?

Consider how the various statements in the *Discipline* about homosexuality generally, and same-gender marriage in particular, relate to each other. Do you feel like the statements send a coherent message, or do they contradict each other in any ways?

Consider Current Teachings on Marriage

Review the section of this chapter titled "Roots of Current Teachings on Marriage." Form small groups of three to four people each, and provide Bibles to assist in the discussion. If possible, have more than one Bible translation available for people to review.

Ask one person in each group to read 1 Corinthians 6:9-20. Check to see whether any notes are included in your Bible(s) for verses 9-10. If you have more than one translation available to you, compare the different words used for the wrongdoers in these verses that are sexual in nature. For example, one translation uses the phrase "male prostitutes,

---

2 Kenneth H. Carter, "Disarm," in *Finding Our Way: Love and Law in The United Methodist Church* (Nashville: Abingdon Press, 2014), 64.

sodomites" (NRSV); another uses "effeminate" and "homosexuals" (NASB); another uses the "men who have sex with men" (NIV); a fourth uses "both participants in same-sex intercourse" (CEB). Ask group members to discuss in their teams the following question: Do these different word choices affect your understanding of what Paul is trying to communicate to the Corinthian church? Why or why not?

As a group, try to summarize the position of those who support The United Methodist Church's current prohibition on same-gender marriage, whether or not you personally support this position. What unanswered questions does this position leave you with?

Consider Teachings in Favor of Same-gender Marriage

Remaining in the small groups formed during the last activity, refer to the section "The Foundation for a Christian Affirmation of Same-gender Marriage." Ask one person in each group to read Matthew 22:34-40. Ask them to discuss in their teams the following questions: What might it mean to love God with all our hearts, and to love our neighbors as ourselves, when it comes to the issue of same-gender marriage?

As a group, try to summarize the position of those who believe that United Methodist clergy and churches should be allowed to perform and host same-gender marriage ceremonies, whether or not you personally support this position. What unanswered questions does this position leave you with?

Discuss How Cultural Context Affects Our Understanding of the Issue

Review the sections of the chapter that examine how the US Supreme Court ruling is affecting the discussion on marriage, as well as the section on The United Methodist Church's global makeup. Ask: As a larger percentage of Americans have become accepting of same-gender marriage, have you seen faith perspectives on this topic shift as well? In what ways?

Ask: What challenges does the global nature of our church present as United Methodists try to find unity around issues of marriage and sexuality? How do you respond to the African Bishops' call in 2016 to unite in solidarity with people who are suffering rather than to be divided by issues of sexuality?

Ask: What do these two sections say to you about the ways we make decisions in The United Methodist Church? What are the benefits of making decisions in this way, and what are the obstacles or drawbacks that arise from doing so?

Examine How Some United Methodists Are Resisting Current Teachings on Marriage

Refer to the section "Resistance to United Methodist Teachings on Same-gender Marriage." On a markerboard, make a list of ways some United Methodists are choosing not to comply with the requirements of the *Discipline* related to same-gender marriage. Ask: What are their reasons for resisting in this way? How do you think these actions are affecting the current discussion of marriage within our denomination? How do you personally respond to these actions?

Consider Outcomes of Performing a Same-gender Marriage

Referring to the section "Possible Outcomes When a Clergyperson Performs a Same-gender Marriage," take a few moments to answer any clarifying questions about how the process for filing and resolving complaints works.

Then review the main examples given in the last section of this chapter about the resolution of cases where same-gender marriages have been performed. Invite the group to consider the comments that Bishops Hoshibata and Palmer have made about church trials. Ask: Do you believe that church trials are furthering productive conversation on issues of sexuality, or cutting that conversation off? From what you have learned about the just resolution process, do you believe that it should be used more often, or do you find it problematic?

Ask: What kinds of processes might help United Methodists who disagree on same-gender marriage find ways to continue to be the church together? What can we as individual United Methodists, as local churches, and as congregations, do to "disarm" and listen better to each other in the midst of deep divisions?

CLOSE the Session

Follow-up from Last Time

In the previous session, the group was given the following instructions to initiate a conversation during the past week.

Seek out someone in your life whom you know has a different view on homosexuality than you do. Ask them how they arrived at their belief. Ask them how they think their belief has been misunderstood. The goal is to just listen and ask questions, not engage in a debate. Pray for this person throughout your week.

Invite group members to share how those conversations went, and what they learned. Remind them to keep praying for the person they spoke to, and invite them to seek to continue the conversation if they so desire.

Pray Together

Close with the following prayer:

Loving God, in these difficult moments for our church, help us to discern what love in action looks like. Forgive us for the times when we have excluded others because of their sexual orientation or because of their beliefs. Let each of us be a small part of determining a way forward, so that we can minister to a hurting world. Amen.

Chapter 3

IS ORDAINING PRACTICING HOMOSEXUALS COMPATIBLE WITH CHRISTIAN TEACHING?

Create Your Own Teaching Plan

Not all of the lesson suggestions below will work for every group. Feel free to edit and make changes that you think will create the best learning experience for your group using the OPEN, EXPLORE, and CLOSE activities.

OPEN the Session

Pray Together

Remind the group of your ground rules for discussion on pages 86–87, then open with the following prayer:

God, author and source of life, giver of all good things, we thank you for calling leaders among us to build up your people. They have often been people we would not have chosen for ourselves—a felon named Moses, a timid Gideon, a non-military Deborah, a fanatical Paul, or a rabble-rousing Jesus. But you continue to call leaders, and you continue to call each of us into greater relationship with you. Give us the wisdom and discernment of your Holy Spirit, the grace to listen with tender ears, and the courage both to lead and to follow. Amen.

Share Favorite Christian Leaders

Say: We all have saints in our lives whom we look up to. Who are some of those people for you who have led the church? What are the characteristics of Christian faith you admire in them?

On a markerboard or large piece of paper, list the names of people your group lifts up. Encourage them to think of great preachers, compassionate leaders, or public figures.

When the class is done, ask them to consider the following questions: How many of these are women? How important was their relationship with their spouse to their witness to you? What other lessons did you learn from these leaders that aren't really about faith—for example, did you learn that pastors should act, dress, or talk a certain way?

Ask: Do you think we should separate the person from his or her message, or is the person part of the message? Why?

EXPLORE the Topic

Discuss Ministry

Read or review the opening sections of this chapter, down through the section titled "The Board of Ordained Ministry." Pay particular attention to the passages from the *Discipline* that are mentioned. On a large sheet of paper or a markerboard, make columns with the following categories: health, maturity, integrity in relationships (write "fidelity and celibacy" below this), social responsibility, and Christian growth.

Ask: When you think of high standards for clergy, what behaviors would you put under these categories? What would your ideal pastor do?

Give the class time to list some behaviors under each column, then ask: Does a person's sexual orientation play a role in his or her ability to uphold these standards? Explain your answer.

Ask: If this group were a Board of Ordained Ministry, and a candidate came before us who was a dynamic and powerful leader—but they were born intersex—would we ordain them? Why or why not?

Discuss the Recent Cases

Read the section of this chapter titled "Historic Challenges." Feel free to find supplementary material or commentary on the cases from Ministry Matters or www.umc.org (see "Helpful Resources and Links," page 87).

Invite the group to summarize the events, ask clarifying questions, and discuss their broad implications. Ask: What strikes you as the most important thing to know about these stories? If you were explaining these stories to someone who didn't go to church, what would you say about them?

Work Through the Quadrilateral

Review the section titled "Using the Quadrilateral to Address the Ordination Question." Say: Though John Wesley never used this framework himself, many United Methodists find it a helpful guide for working through questions about Christian teaching. In this section, we're not talking about homosexuality in general, but specifically what we believe about ordination.

Create four columns on a large sheet of paper or a markerboard, then label them Scripture, Tradition, Reason, and Experience.

Scripture

First, assign pairs or teams to look at some of the Scriptures cited in the "Scripture" section of the essay: Exodus 3:1–4:18, Leviticus 9, Jeremiah 1:4-10, Amos 7:14-15, 1 Timothy 2:11-15, Luke 24:1-11, Acts 2:18, Matthew 23:1-5, 13-15. Encourage them to note anything of relevance about how God calls leaders or what God (or the church) looks for in leaders. Ask the readers to report back to the group what they found. Make a list of questions or relevant points.

Tradition

There are two stories under the section titled "Tradition": Requirements for Methodist Preachers, and the Ordination of Women. Break into two teams and ask the groups to discuss these stories and their relevance to the ordination of "self-avowed practicing homosexuals." On separate sheets of paper or two sides of a markerboard, write down the relevant points of the stories and the connections your group draws.

Reason

There are two main ideas in the "Reason" section of this chapter. The first is that the church community participates in the calling of individuals by guiding and confirming their call. The second is that those who are ordained enter into a covenant to uphold the *Discipline*, but the *Discipline* itself includes provisions for making changes to it.

Invite the group to read or summarize the "Reason" section, then ask the following questions: How do you understand the relationship between God's calling of an individual and the community's role in affirming or guiding that call? What tensions do you see between the larger church community and the more local instances of community such as local churches and Boards of Ordained Ministry?

Ask: What tensions do you see between accountability to a covenant and to one's conscience? When is disobedience an acceptable or effective way of advocating for change, and when is it not?

Ask: Do you find these arguments convincing? Why or why not? Do you find their counterarguments convincing? Why or why not? Are your denomination's beliefs and practices important to you? How would you respond to someone who told you that you would be better off in a leadership role that you hadn't envisioned for yourself?

Experience

The best way to discuss experience is to bring in someone who has actually been through the ordination process to discuss it, or to bring in LGBTQ clergy from another denomination to discuss their own experience and their ministry. Be aware that asking persons to share their experience can be presumptuous on the part of people who are not LGBTQ. It is best to ask someone with whom you have a friendly relationship rather than to ask a stranger to do the hard work of educating your group (especially if they are not entirely sympathetic). If this is possible, invite someone to your group session to have a discussion with your group.

CLOSE the Session

Pray Together

Close your session with the following prayer:

God who called us into being, called us into relationship with you, and called us into community—give to us the transforming love of your Spirit, that we may be made more Christ-like, both in our personal conduct and in our relationship with others. Send us leaders who will challenge us and help us grow. Amen.

Chapter 4

WHERE ARE WE NOW?

Create Your Own Teaching Plan

Keeping in mind your group members and your group time, choose from among the OPEN, EXPLORE, and CLOSE activities to plan this session.

OPEN the Session

Pray together

After persons have gathered, invite them into silence and light a candle, sharing that the light in the midst of the group is a sign of Christ's presence among us. Read Ephesians 2:14 aloud: "Christ is our peace. He made both Jews and Gentiles into one group. With his body, he broke down the barrier of hatred that divided us."

Then offer the following prayer or one of your own:

Lord, we pray that our shoulders
    will not be lent to one more wheel
        whose work amounts to vanity.
The good gift of our strength,
    such as it is,
    is too easily wasted on
        projects of our own design.
We want a cause that
        calls forth our faith, our best, our all,
    a labor that
        is fed by a native trust in you,
            so long neglected.
Help us not to offer gifts
    that cost us nothing. Amen.

EXPLORE the Topic

Review United Methodist Structure

This chapter refers to a lot of bodies in the United Methodist structure. Before beginning the session, prepare cards for each of the following and include the brief definition for each:

- **General Conference**: The global gathering of United Methodists that normally meets once every four years. Made up of an equal number of lay and clergy delegates, this is the legislative body of The United Methodist Church. The last General Conference was held in 2016 in Portland, Oregon. A special General Conference has been called for February 2019 in Saint Louis, Missouri.

- **Jurisdictional Conference**: One of the five regional conferences within the United States whose most prominent duty is to elect and assign bishops for their region.

- **Central Conference:** The organizational unit for United Methodists outside the United States that corresponds to the Jurisdictional Conference in the United States.

- **Annual Conference**: A regional organizational unit of The United Methodist Church, presided over by a bishop.

- **Bishop**: An ordained clergy person, elected by a jurisdictional conference (in the United States) or by a central conference (outside the United States) and assigned to lead an episcopal area made up of one or more annual conferences.

- **Judicial Council**: The nine-member body that is charged with interpreting the constitution of The United Methodist Church.

Distribute the cards to volunteers and ask them to read them aloud. After each one is read, post it on the wall or on a large piece of paper so that they can all be seen throughout the session.

Invite participants to describe the role that each body has played in the church's debate over human sexuality, based on what they have read in chapter 4 and in previous chapters of this book.

Report on the Commission on a Way Forward

Read the section of chapter 4 entitled "The Commission on a Way Forward emerges from the 2016 General Conference." Imagine that you are a reporter trying to get the basic facts on the Commission. Answer the following questions as a group:

- What is the Commission and what is its purpose?
- Who commissioned it, and who is on it?
- When was it formed, and when will its work return to the General Conference?
- Where was it formed?
- Why was it formed?

Debate the Positions of the Sugar Packet Model

Read the section of the chapter entitled, "A Methodist Middle." Using the categories described in Rev. Tom Berlin's model, divide the group into four smaller groups, with each one assigned one of the categories from the model. Persons should be randomly assigned; their category may or may not reflect their individual beliefs. Ask each group to take its assigned category and discuss how they might be feeling about the current debates over human sexuality in The UMC if they were identified with this group.

Ask them to read through the sections of the chapter entitled "The Election and Consecration of Karen Oliveto," "The Wesleyan Covenant Association," and "African Responses," and to reflect on how they would respond to the events described in each from the perspective of their assigned category. (For example: as a traditionalist non-compatibilist, how would I view the election of Bishop Karen Oliveto?)

After allowing some time for discussion within the groups, come back together as a whole group and have each group share their reflections. Ask: What are your observations about the exercise of entering into another perspective (if you were in a group that didn't correspond to your own perspective)?

Study Scripture Together

This chapter includes several passages of Scripture that focus on the theme of unity. Psalm 133 and Ephesians 2:11-22 both touch on this. Read through the Ephesians passage together and discuss what its central point or main idea is. Ask: What did it mean to its original hearers? What might it mean for us today? If we took this passage seriously, what would have to change about our notion of unity?

In the section of the chapter entitled "It's Time to Stop Destroying the Couch," the Rev. Tom Berlin refers to "walking together loosely" as a model of connection that doesn't mean "coming to agreement." Ask: How possible is it for us to walk together loosely on questions of human sexuality? How would our connection as a church have to change for us to accept this model? Ask: How would our connection as a church have to change for us to move forward in a different way, such as making a change for the whole denomination or having one or more groups separate?

Commit to Act

Read the section of the chapter entitled "A Time for Conversation and New Community." This final section asks what we can do in this time before the next General Conference. Discuss the opportunities of this season and how your group might foster deeper conversations among yourselves and others in your faith community. Evaluate how your own views and your sense of connection to others in the group have changed through the course of this study. What other actions might you commit to in order to model new expressions of Christian community?

CLOSE the Session

Pray Together

As a closing act of worship, invite participants to center themselves by looking at the lit candle among them once again. Then offer this prayer in closing.

In a season of discernment,
as your church, in which we have met you,
        meets across divides,
    as a commission confers on a Way Forward,
    as we hunger for a way beyond our walls,
Pour out your Spirit, as we say,
    on us gathered here.
By your Spirit, we say
    make us one with Christ,
    one with each other,
    and one in ministry to all the world.
Until, in your Spirit,
    the blurred and blinding chaos
    of this broken world and church
    resolves into a feast
and you are host and Lord. Amen.

MEET THE WRITERS

Jill M. Johnson is a freelance writer and Director of Inviting Ministries at Bethany United Methodist Church in Austin, Texas.

Dave Barnhart is pastor of Saint Junia United Methodist Church in Birmingham, Alabama.

Rebekah Jordan Gienapp is an ordained deacon in the Memphis Conference.

Alex Joyner is the District Superintendent of the United Methodist churches on Virginia's Eastern Shore. He is an author, most recently of *A Space for Peace in the Holy Land: Listening to Modern Israel & Palestine* [Englewood Books, 2014]. He writes regularly on rural life and ministry on the Heartlands blog: www.alexjoyner.com.

CPSIA information can be obtained
at www.ICGtesting.com
Printed in the USA
LVHW02s1746200818
587328LV00003B/3/P